The Big Book of
SPY STUFF

THE BIG BOOK OF

SPY STUFF

BART KING

ILLUSTRATIONS BY RUSSELL MILLER

GIBBS SMITH
TO ENRICH AND INSPIRE HUMANKIND

TO THE MOST CUNNING, DECEPTIVE, AND DEADLY MAN I'VE EVER MET: JARED SMITH

Manufactured in Baoan, Shenzhen, China in January 2011 by Toppan

First Edition
15 14 13 12 11   5 4 3 2 1
Text © 2011 by Bart King
Illustrations © 2011 by Russell Miller

This book contains material that is interesting and entertaining. (At least, that's what I like to tell myself.) But as it's about espionage and other anti-social activities, remember that you assume all legal responsibility for all your actions. Please obey all laws and respect everyone else's rights. And just to be clear, both the publisher and I are disclaiming any liability from your actions.

   I have relied on my own experience as an intelligence agent as well as many different sources for this book, and I have done my best to check facts and to give credit where it is due. In the event that any material is incorrect or has been used without proper permission, please contact me care of the publisher so that it can be properly amended.

Published by
Gibbs Smith
P.O. Box 667
Layton, Utah 84041

1.800.835.4993 orders
www.gibbs-smith.com

Design by Black Eye Design
Produced by Renee Bond

Gibbs Smith books are printed on either recycled, 100% post-consumer waste, FSC-certified papers or on paper produced from a sustainable PEFC-certified forest/controlled wood source. Learn more at www.pefc.org.

Library of Congress Cataloging-in-Publication Data

King, Bart, 1962-
The big book of spy stuff / Bart King ; illustrations by Russell Miller. — 1st ed.
     p. cm.
Includes bibliographical references.
ISBN 978-1-4236-1874-4
1. Spies—Juvenile literature. 2. Espionage—Juvenile literature.
3. Espionage—Humor. I. Miller, Russell. II. Title.
UB270.5.K55 2010
327.12—dc22
                                        2010035248

TOP SECRET

CONTENTS

DANGER
Is My Nickname

Hey, can you hold still for a second? This book is electronically scanning your right eye to figure out your security clearance. (You've heard of e-books, right?)

While it's doing that, let me tell you about my spy credentials. First, I am an expert in *sabotage* (SAB-uh-taj), the art of destroying or damaging things for spy-ish reasons. My list of accomplishments includes derailing a toy train and blowing up a pumpkin.

Furthermore, I can kill with my bare feet (although I prefer not to step on caterpillars if I can help it). And while I can't confirm or deny any more details on my background, I *can* tell you that I'm a writer . . . and trust me, writers are spies! The difference is that a writer wants to discover secrets and then share them with *everybody.* A spy wants to discover secrets and share them with *nobody* (or sell them to a high-paying client).

Hey, it looks like this book's eye-scan is done, and—uh-oh: you're not cleared for *any* top secret material at all! That's too bad. So please stop reading right now.

Did you hear what I said?

Well, I guess *THAT'S* not going to work.

Wait! By continuing to read despite my threats, you've proven your interest in discovering hidden secrets. And that's good enough for me! After all, "learning secrets" is why most spies get into spying. Because being "one up" on everyone else is pretty cool.

Of course, not all spies want to be cool. Some just don't have any choice! For example, in 1993 a man named Bin Wu was arrested for trying to smuggle night-vision equipment out of the United States and into China. But here's what's amazing: Bin Wu *hated* the Chinese government! In fact, Bin Wu had been arrested for protesting against China's policies. After Bin Wu was arrested, he was given a choice: either work as a secret agent for China or go to prison for a long time. (Guess which one he picked?)

SPIES: THE EXCEPTION TO THE RULE

Guess what? Many people automatically dislike anyone who has the word "agent" in his or her job title. Literary agent, talent agent, chemical agent . . . we hate 'em *all!* Do you know the *only* exception to this? *Secret* agents!

According to this book's electronic scan, you're also an honest person. So maybe you don't think you're cut out for spying. Think again! If you've read this far, you're almost ready to trade in your goody-two-shoes for spy boots with poison gas canisters hidden in their heels. And then you'll be ready to do something *really* glamorous, like writing up spy reports.

Nobody knows what the first spy report was. But the oldest one we know of was written 4,000 years ago on a clay tablet somewhere in what is now Iraq. (It was a secret plan to watch for fire signals on the Euphrates River.)

My guess is that the *actual* oldest spy report was from hundreds of thousands of years ago and went something like this:

"Commander Thok, I am ready to give my report."

"Go ahead, Agent Boomp."

"I saw Reegu collecting shells!"

"Good work!" *pause* "Uh, why do you think Reegu was doing this?"

"Maybe he wants to start using the shells for money?"

"But that would totally destroy our current system of buying and selling items using very small rocks!"

"Perhaps he just thinks seashells are pretty."

"They are, aren't they? I especially like the curly ones with the blue insides." *pause* "But we should probably hit Reegu over the head with something hard just to be safe."

As we have learned from the cavemen, spying is very exciting! It combines danger, secrecy, and the potential for making *really* big mistakes. And in modern times, spies get to wear cool sunglasses!

WHY SPY?

But cool sunglasses alone don't explain spying. The fact is that every nation wants to protect its borders and its citizens. Here are three ways nations can do this:

1. Make treaties with other countries.
2. Have a military.
3. Spy!

While I don't know for certain that cave people used spies, ancient civilizations did. For example, Greek mythology had the story of the demigod named Prometheus (pro-MEETH-ee-us). He stole secret technology (namely, fire) from the head god, Zeus (zoos). Then Prometheus gave this classified information to the humans. Finally, after getting caught, Prometheus was sentenced to having his liver eaten by an eagle. Just like spies today!

And in between screams, I'll bet Prometheus would have agreed with the words of ancient Chinese leader Sun Tzu: "An army without secret agents is like a man without eyes and ears."

Hey, did you hear that? "*Eyes* and ears." So *that's* why spies need sunglasses (and earpieces).

Okay, now we understand why nations have spies. But I have to point out something before going onward. People like me love to learn about the secrets and failures of spies throughout history. But for every flub or mistake that a spy or spy agency makes, there are countless times when they save lives, foil enemy plots, and otherwise do exactly what people *hope* they will do.

So why don't we hear more about spies saving the day? Because these successes are SECRET! The CIA (Central Intelligence Agency) even has an unofficial motto: "Our failures are publicized. Our successes are not." So don't think that all spies are dangerous, bumbling nincompoops... because only some of them are.

And the spies who are really good at their jobs are the ones you'll NEVER hear about. (Like me!)

"ETHICAL ISSUES"?
What Are Those?

I'll admit it. This book is steeped in treachery, lies, and deception.[1] Look, a spy *has* to deceive other people. It's even in the job description: "Spy—a person who secretly collects information on an enemy or competitor." (One former agent told me that a three-word motto for his job was "Befriend and betray.")

In order for a spy to secretly collect information, he or she will use many, many forms of trickery, starting with lying! In fact, you could say that a spy is a *professional liar*. But while you may believe lying is always wrong, sometimes telling a lie can prevent something awful from happening. This means that lying and deception can be necessary—and even *good*! Here's what I mean:

Bad deception—A spy who's working for a private agency sneaks his way into a job with a corporation. There he learns of a new, top secret cure for baldness. The spy steals

---

1. It's awesome!

the formula and sells it to a rival corporation for millions of dollars. Meanwhile, the original inventor of the baldness cure (my hero!) doesn't get a penny.

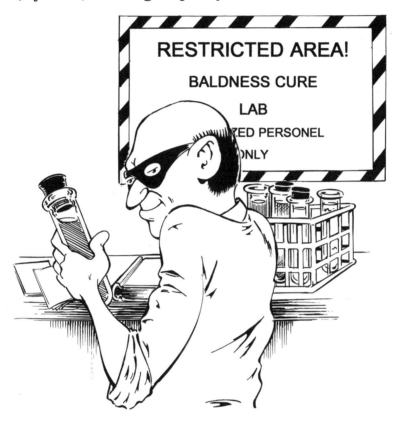

Good deception—Using a secret identity, a government spy sneaks his way into a terrorist group. There he learns of an upcoming attack on his country. He warns the authorities, and the lives of innocent people are saved!

But the lines between bad and good deception are not always so clear. The world of spying can be so tricky and murky, it's been called a "wilderness of mirrors." So that makes having a strong moral sense of right and wrong one of the most important traits of a spy. Of course, "right" and "wrong" can depend on a person's point of view and what country they come from.

During the Revolutionary War, American agent Nathan Hale (p. 237) had a friend who thought spying was *always* disgraceful. Hale said something like this to him: "Anything done for the good of the majority is honorable because it's necessary." And this leads us to the age-old question: When does the *end* (the outcome, or result) justify the *means* (the method, or spying)? Put another way, what makes it okay to do something illegal (the *means)* for the sake of helping a nation (the *end*)?

IMAGINARY CASE IN POINT 1

The neighboring nation of Piddlehinton is on good relations with your homeland. But your spymaster informs you that Piddlehinton might have plans to invade your country. If you're willing to go on the mission, you can go to Piddlehinton and steal those invasion plans!

Should you go? Is that the right thing to do?

If you say "yes," that means you would be committing a crime of theft against a country that has done no harm to yours. In fact, you'd be stealing something from one of your country's allies.

But let's say you go through with this theft anyway. As you stick the secret invasion plans down your black turtleneck, a security guard shows up. What would you be willing to do to protect the invasion plans?

a. Surrender

b. Try to knock out the guard

c. Use your ninja throwing stars on the guard.

If you chose *b* or *c*, you'd be attacking a person who is trying to stop a crime. Uncool!

Of course, we could turn this around. What if a spy from Piddlehinton were trying to steal top secret invasion plans from *your* country. Remember, this spy would be doing exactly what you were going to do!

Would you try to stop him? Capture him? Throw ninja stars at him?

IMAGINARY CASE IN POINT II

Ooh, I have an even tougher dilemma! Let's say your country and Piddlehinton are already at war. War is hard on more than just the soldiers. And you've heard that some of the people of Piddlehinton have been dying of disease.

Through your spy network, you catch word that Piddlehinton agents are smuggling supplies into the country. While investigating, you find a group of women and children that are about to cross the border into Piddlehinton.

At first, this seems okay, but then you notice that all of the children have dolls. You've always been secretly afraid of dolls, so you have an agent take a closer look at them. The agent finds that all of the children's dolls are filled with . . . medicine!

What do you do? On the one hand, this medicine is headed to an enemy country. On the other hand, it will probably be used to help innocent people. Are you going to take the medicine away and arrest a bunch of women and children?

This actually *has* happened before. During the Civil War, secret agents smuggled medicine into the South using dolls. These were sometimes found by Union soldiers, who had to decide what to do with the dolls. (Playing with them was *not* an option).

Do you see how complex the world of spying can be? It's a BIG complex world, too, because every single nation has spies. Even Vatican City, a country with fewer than 1,000 citizens, has at least one spy!

Nations usually send their spies to both friendly and unfriendly countries. That's because a friendly country might have better secrets than an enemy. And there is always the chance that a friendly country might become an *unfriendly* one . . . so, better safe than sorry!

The United States and many other nations have secret agents in every *other* nation in the world. And all U.S. agents have permission to spy wherever they are, *except* for the American agents in Great Britain, Canada, New Zealand, and Australia. These countries (and the U.S.) are known as the Five Eye allies, and they have a "you don't spy on us, we don't spy on you" agreement with each other.

IT'S A TRICKY PROBLEM!

It's hard to prove that friendly countries really aren't spying on each other. As one agent said, "How would you verify it—by spying?"

Most nations in the world accept the fact that CIA agents are running around in their country. And in many cases, they're happy to have the spies! That's because CIA agents might find out some good information and then *share* it with those countries. The United States often returns the favor by allowing foreign spies within its borders.

OUR ROLE MODEL: SIR FRANCIS WALSINGHAM

Is it even possible to be a good person and also a good spy? Maybe. Sir Francis Walsingham (c. 1530–1590) created England's first spy agency. In his 20 years of leading a team of more than 70 secret agents, Walsingham protected Queen Elizabeth from assassins and England from invasion by Spain.

In all the time Walsingham ran the spy agency, he never once used it for his own benefit. In fact, Walsingham paid his spies himself, out of his own pocket. (Trust me, that's impressive.) So, although Sir Francis Walsingham cheated, lied, and spied for his nation, he was actually an honest man!

We can see that even in the world of spying, there are rules. And that brings us to TRAITORS. A traitor is someone who betrays his country. Someone like John Walker. He was an officer in the U.S. Navy who sold over 250,000 secret documents to Russia.

When Walker was arrested in 1985, it seemed clear that he was a traitor. Not only did he sell his nation's secrets to a rival nation, he hadn't even been recruited. Walker just walked into to the Russian embassy and asked if they needed secrets! (Walker was given life in prison.)

Then there's the case of Jonathan Pollard, a U.S. intelligence officer who stole more than one *million* pages of classified material. Pollard sold those papers to a nation that is a FRIEND of the United States, namely, Israel. Is that just as bad as what Walker did? (Pollard was also given life in prison.)

What do we call a person who gives his nation's secrets to the *public*? In 2010, a U.S. Army intelligence analyst named Bradley Manning was arrested for leaking a video. The video showed the crews of two American attack helicopters firing at a group of mostly unarmed people in Iraq. (Eleven people were killed in the attack, including a news photographer.)

Manning gave this video and thousands of secret messages to a website called WikiLeaks. (It's an online source of information that governments and corporations would prefer to keep secret.) Manning wanted ALL of this material to be made public. Was it because he wanted to betray his country? Or did he have an honest desire for people to know the truth? (This kind of person is called a "whistleblower.")

If he was, in fact, a whistleblower, does that make Manning a traitor or a hero? Or something in between?

NOT OUR ROLE MODEL

From the early 1970s to 2007, Monzer al-Kassar was the man to see for anyone looking for guns or explosives. It didn't matter who you were or what you wanted the weapons for—if you had money, al-Kassar would sell them to you.

When asked how he could work with hostile spies, terrorists and criminals, al-Kassar answered, *"How do I know who's good and who's bad? The bad people for you may be the good people for me."*

Hoo-boy. It's pretty clear that Monzer al-Kassar is bad for almost everybody!

HIGH-TECH
Espionage!

Espionage (pronounced ESS-pee-uh-nahjh) means "spying" or "gathering intelligence." It's a very cool word, so use it as much as possible. Sure, some agents like the word "tradecraft" instead. (It means the same thing.) Bor-ing! While the world of "warcraft" *is* impressive, "tradecraft" sounds like you're bartering for handmade vests.

Anyway, sitting down to write about computer espionage, I wondered, "How will this apply to most people?"

Then I typed in my password to log on to the computer. Wow, I must have taken some Vitamin Duh this morning!

Computer espionage is something that affects EVERYONE—even those three people in South Carolina who don't have computers yet. That's because we all have to protect ourselves from hackers. Yes, passwords *should* keep our online accounts safe. But I've learned that people often pick passwords so lame, any toddler could figure them out!

Here's what I mean. This is one of the most popular computer passwords of all time:

Do you see that? It's the word *password* spelled backwards. Wow! This is even cleverer than just using the word *password* for a password. And guess what? Whether spelled backward or forward, *password* is one of the most popular passwords around!

Researchers study the passwords people use. Here is a list of the some of the most common ones:

123456—One percent of all computer users use this or another series of numbers for their password.

654321—Backwards thinking.

iloveyou—Sweet but should read "ilovegettinghacked."

abcdef—Or any similar letter sequence.

abc123—Ooh! Getting tricky!

[person's first name]—Because it's so simple, no one will figure it out! (Unless they try.)

qwerty—Look where these keys are on the keyboard.

11111—I just threw my head back and laughed.

0—Yes, the whole password is the number o. (That's just really sad.)

tigger—Don't look at me, I'm just reporting this stuff!

As a spy, you owe it to your profession to have a better password than "tigger." Try to combine something RANDOM with a PATTERN you can remember. For example, start with a short kooky phrase that you can't forget, like "spiesR1st."

Then try combining that basic password with the different names of the sites you go to. So if you visit Facebook, the password there could be "facebookspiesR1st." Also, adding a capital letter and an * symbol makes a password *thousands* of times more difficult for hackers to figure out!

Of course, if you think I'm going to help you STEAL passwords, think again! Oh wait, this IS a book about spying, isn't it? Maybe you should know these strategies so you can protect yourself from password theft! Fair enough.

PASSWORD THEFT

One of the best ways to snag someone's password is to just *look while* a person logs on to his computer.

I'm kidding—and I'm not. Try to find innocent reasons to loiter around a person's computer when they log on for the day. The key is that the first number of times you do this, you make it clear that you're *not* looking at what the person is doing. But over time, you'll be able to sneak a peek at the keystrokes of the password. Just try to get *one* keystroke ("p"!), and then make a note of it. Skip a day, then try to get another keystroke to their password on your next try!

Naturally, you're not going to learn the whole password quickly. This could take years! Maybe even weeks. But with patience, you'll get there. Agents call this the "Elephant Technique" because it requires patience. (Its name is taken from an old joke.[1])

HOT TIP!

To protect yourself from just this sort of thing, try to have a password that takes *two* hands to type. (It's harder for spies to track all ten fingers.) And if anyone makes a point of hanging around while you're logging on, have your pet elephant step on them.

---

1. Q. How do you eat a whole elephant? A. One bite at a time.

HACKING, COMPUTER ESPIONAGE, AND CYBER-WAR

You know what? The Elephant Technique sounds like a *ton* of work. Maybe you should just hire a hacker instead! Because when it comes to computer espionage, there are millions of professional hackers out there, trying to sneak into computers all over the planet. These hackers aren't just trying to sneak onto Facebook pages. Each day, the average U.S. military officer working in the Pentagon can get up to 5,000 hack attempts on his computer. And military networks get probed hundreds of thousands of times daily!

What can happen if the enemy hackers succeed? Let me tell you a little story:

In 2007, Israel's leaders were suspicious of a secret nuclear plant that its enemy, Syria, was building. But Israel's military couldn't just fly jets in and bomb the plant. After all, Syria has really good radar and an air defense that could shoot down any attacking jets.

Instead, Israeli hackers took over the computers that ran Syria's air defenses. The hackers programmed the air defense computers to show that everything was normal and just fine. And then, Israel just flew its jets in and blew up the nuclear plant!

What a fun story! Now, enjoy reading about some of the different goals that high-tech hackers use.

CYBER-ESPIONAGE: Sneaking on to a computer to STEAL information.

Example: In 2007, a series of computer attacks on U.S. government agencies resulted in the loss of 10 to 20 terabytes of data. That's more data than is stored in every library in whatever city you live in! (Experts think the attack came from China.)

CYBER-SABOTAGE: Trying to sneak into a computer or server to DESTROY its contents.

Example: In 2008, a troublemaker sprinkled a bunch of thumb drives around the parking lot of a U.S. military base in Tampa, Florida. Naturally, somebody got curious and picked up one of the thumb drives. *"Gee, I wonder why these are here?"*

Then that person went to a computer on the military base and stuck the thumb drive into a computer. (*"Guess I'll find out!"*) And then the thumb drive infected thousands of military computers with a malicious (mean and evil) software that screwed up everything! *"Oops!"*

CYBER-ZOMBIES: Hacker-spies can TAKE OVER a group of computers, combine them into a network, and then command them to send out viruses or commit other mischief. The infected computers are called "zombie computers." Their network is a "robot network" or "botnet."

Example: North American security experts recently exposed a huge computer espionage group in China. The group was nicknamed "The Shadow Network." During their observations, the experts watched in amazement as Chinese hackers infected computers in over a hundred different countries and turned them into a global network of botnets.

These zombie computers were controlled remotely and made to report to servers in China. Among other things, the botnets snuck into the MOST top secret computers of India's government, where they stole reports on Indian missile systems and learned military secrets about India's allies, including the United States.

CYBER-WARFARE: When two nations go to war in the 21st century, the *first* thing that happens is their *computers* start attacking each other. Because, while it takes time to launch jets and fire missiles, a computer attack can happen at the speed of light!

Example: In 2009, the nations of Georgia and Russia went to war. Before the tanks started to roll, Georgia's government computers were attacked. Hackers shut down Georgia's media, banking, and government computers. What kind of hackers? Russian hackers!

What the Russians did is called a "DDoS" (Distributed Denial of Service). That's what happens when an enemy sends millions of "fake" visitors to a website, causing it to crash. This can be a pretty big deal if it's a government website that is crucial for communications!

CYBER-WARRIORS RULE

Because of this new type of cyber-hacking, the U.S. military created a whole new branch of defense called the Cyber Command (a.k.a. CYBERCOM). Agents working there call themselves "cyber-warriors," which we can all agree is the coolest job title ever. (It's much better than "hacker.")

What do U.S. cyber-warriors worry about? China! Most experts think that China has more cyber-warriors than any other country. Heck, there is even a Chinese university that teaches courses like "network attack technology"! Another thing the Chinese government does is look for kids who have been caught hacking. Then it *hires* the hackers!

MY NAME IS BOND . . . BUT WHAT SHOULD MY SCREEN NAME BE?

In 2010, British intelligence agents faced their greatest foe ever. Sure, they had spied against Muslim terrorists and Russian meanies. But this time, they were up against a tougher foe: computers!

In order to improve computer skills among staff, the British Security Service began firing older agents and hiring younger people with technology backgrounds.

So has the "James Bond generation" of rickety spies been retired because they can't log on to Twitter?

Yes!

FUN FACT

When John McCain and Barack Obama ran for the U.S. presidency, *both* of their campaign headquarters were hacked into from computers in China.

In China, the government controls all computer networks. So when a Chinese official says, "The Chinese government considers hacking as a cancer to the whole society," you just have to smile! That is, unless you work for Google. You see, in 2010, Google pulled all operations out of China because it got tired of hackers constantly trying to sneak into its computer systems. These were almost certainly government-sponsored attacks. One clue was that the hackers were *very* interested in any people working for human rights in China.

Oh, wait! I haven't told you of the greatest cyber-outrage against humanity ever! Last year, a three-year-old boy armed with a jar of peanut butter smeared goo over my laptop's keyboard. While I cannot prove anything, I suspect Chinese involvement.

One more thing. To keep on the cutting edge, the United States began a competition called the Cyber Challenge. It's a national talent search for high school cyber-warriors. Young hackers compete against each other in cyber-competitions.

The 2009 Cyber Challenge was won by a 17-year-old named Michael Coppola. To win, he hacked into the main Cyber Challenge computer and added points to his own score!

Was that cheating? Oh, please! The judges loved it. As Michael said, "It's cheating, but it's like the entire game is cheating." (Something tells me he'll make a good cyber-warrior!)

WIKIPEDIA IS FOR AMATEURS

Do spies ever use Wikipedia? Sort of. American intelligence professionals have their *own* version of it called Intellipedia. It's a place for U.S. agents, spymasters, and experts to create and edit intelligence entries. But what if you're a CIA agent who's working on a project, and you'd like to ask for help from other agencies? Luckily, there's MySpace—or the spy version of it, which is known as A-Space. That's where a CIA agent in Virginia can get help from an NSA agent in Seattle!

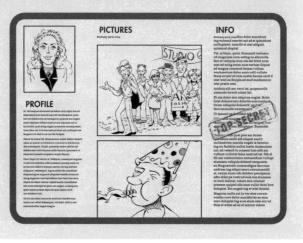

Hey, imagine that you could track all of the phone calls, emails, Twitter feeds, IMs (instant messages, for those of you who are suffering abbreviation overload), and text messages in the world. Impossible? Not really! You see, there are billions of these messages every day, and they contain an untold wealth of intelligence.

That's where the tip-top secret Project ECHELON comes in. This program is so secret, most governments won't even talk about it. It is rumored to use a network of supercomputers to go through *all* of the world's electronic communications looking for important details.

Ooh, that means something like this could happen:

Enemy Spy (is hanging with his buds)

Project ECHELON: Are you in an apartment?

ES: Uh, maybe.

PE: Is the apartment in Berlin?

ES: Not even close.

PE: We located your laptop's signal there an hour ago.

ES: Eep!

PE: Why don't we come over and hang out with you! We have a lot to talk about.

ES: (goes off-line)

SECRET AGENT
Tool Kits & Self-Defense!

Hey, you're still here? Just hang on a second while I put my Swiss Army knife down. I have to be careful with it, because this isn't just ANY pocketknife. What makes it special is that in addition to the usual attachments (retractable ballpoint pen, wrench, flashlight), it has a memory chip (flash drive) that self-destructs if anyone tampers with it. (Really!)

The pocketknife also has a fingerprint identifier with a heat sensor. That means the memory chip will only work if my finger is still *attached* to my body. If an enemy agent were to cut off my finger and try to use it to access my memory chip, the memory chip would self-destruct!

Of course, if someone cut my finger off, I probably wouldn't be that worried about my memory chip.[1]

Anyway, this chapter is about the things a spy should keep in his or her toolkit. One thing a spy *shouldn't* have in there is a joke book. Spies do not joke around! That's because they are often in tense situations that aren't very funny.

Worse, spies often have to work in tense *nations* that aren't very funny. You know, the kind of countries that have traditions of mean dictators, ruthless police officers, and really bad television shows.

These are the type of countries that might have jokes like this one from Russia. It's a joke about people who tell jokes:

"There are people who TELL jokes. Then there are people who COLLECT jokes. And finally, there are people who COLLECT the people who TELL jokes."

Heheh . . . ouch.

---

1. On the plus side, clipping my nails wouldn't take as long!

Now picture this real-life situation:

A Russian agent enters a Moscow movie theater. The theater is showing the premiere of a Hollywood blockbuster. As the film starts, the Russian puts on the coolest spy gadget that's ever been created—night-vision goggles!

As the agent looks around, it's pretty clear he isn't interested in watching the movie. Nope, he's trying to catch a *pirate*.

Ah-ha! Our agent's night vision reveals that someone is taping the blockbuster—in other words, a criminal is making a movie of the movie! This is known as a "pirated" copy, and while it might make a *LOT* of money for the movie pirates, it will also cost the movie studio millions of dollars in lost sales.

Our agent is going to bust the pirate. And in this case, the movie being pirated was one of the *Pirates of the Caribbean* films. You see, Disney hired a private spy agency to take care of just this sort of problem. (This particular agency is run by retired Russian intelligence officers and policemen.) So the agent caught a pirate making a pirated version of a pirate movie!

I told you night-vision goggles are the best! Hey, speaking of films, based on my experience watching spy movies, the coolest gadgets get invented when someone says, "This is a crazy idea, but it just might work." And it turns out there's a U.S. government agency devoted to *exactly* that kind of approach. It's known as . . .

THE DEPARTMENT OF MAD SCIENTISTS!

Okay, the department's official name is the Defense Advanced Research Projects Agency (DARPA), but its nickname is more accurate. After all, according to DARPA's director, the people working there are an "elite army of futuristic techno geeks." That's because DARPA is constantly looking for scientists and researchers doing things so crazy that nobody else will believe in them. When DARPA was originally created, its mission was to prevent the United States from ever being "surprised" by a cool invention that another country was working on. The way DARPA avoids being surprised is by inventing surprises of its *own*!

What kinds of surprises? Well, most of them are secret, but here are a few things the Mad Scientists have invented:

- the computer mouse
- GPS systems for navigation
- "stealth" jets that radar can't detect
- language translators
- cars that drive themselves in traffic
- artificial limbs that look and act like real ones

You've definitely heard of another one of DARPA's inventions: the Internet! You knew the Mad Scientists invented the World Wide Web, right? Yep, back in the 1970s, the "Net" was a project designed to help with military communication. And here's the beauty of DARPA's mad scientists: they share their inventions whenever they can. Whenever DARPA comes up with an invention that will help society, they *give it away*. So, we ALL get to use the Internet. Thanks, DARPA!

Before I share more information about gizmos and technology, I have to tell you about the **Moscow Rules.** These are rules that CIA agents came up with while working in Moscow, which used to be the hardest place in the world to do some good spying. One of the Moscow Rules is this: "Technology will always let you down."[2]

If you've ever had a computer or a Swiss Army knife freeze up on you, you know what I'm talking about. And that's why a good spy knows there is no substitute for human intelligence, or HUMINT.

There are also a number of low-tech supplies that will prove useful to have for gathering information, or what we spies call "intelligence." Check around and see if you have any or most of these:

---

2. Other Moscow Rules include "Any operation can be cancelled" and "Moscow is really cold."

Sunglasses: wraparounds or mirrored pilot glasses are the spy's preferred models.

Lock-picking device: also known as a bent paperclip.

Old cell phone: save your cell phones. With a battery and a chip, they are the perfect way to store important numbers or messages. (Remember, you can write things in the address bars). And you can easily hide something like a note inside a cell phone, even if it doesn't have a battery or chip!

Binoculars or mini-telescope: I don't have to explain this, do I?

Camera: In the old days of film, cameras were developed so a spy could take a picture of a whole page of secret information and then reduce it on film to the size of a dot. These were called "micro-dot cameras." Since everyone knows about these, you should get either a polka-dot camera or a micro-stripe camera instead. Both of these will catch your enemies unaware!

But at least have a digital camera (or a cell phone with built-in camera) with you at all times.

Dabs of wax (or chewing gum): One of the easiest ways to steal a paper is to dab the back of a clipboard or folder with bits of modeling clay or magician's wax. As you're walking and talking, casually set your clipboard down on the document you want. Then pick it up!

Fake coins: Spies have been known to keep poisonous suicide pills in hollow coins. That way, if captured, a really dedicated spy can end his life before he's tortured into giving away a national secret. I do something similar: I carry Flintstones vitamins with me in a special container. If I'm captured, I will immediately eat one so that the vitamin can strengthen my resolve not to give away secrets.

While these supplies are all well and good, how do you carry all of them around? Many agents wear cargo pants and also a sport jacket or large shirt that they *customize* with additional pockets. For example, the coat below has a number of inside pockets:

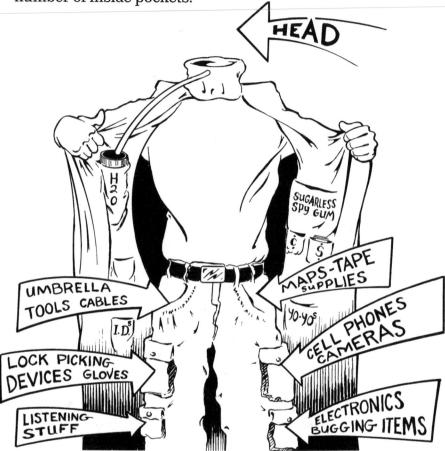

WEAPONS AND SELF-DEFENSE!

Because of your dangerous profession, the time may come when you have to defend yourself. But even though spies don't like to attract attention, defending yourself can be a noisy business. For instance, I go into a karate crouch if attacked. Next, I freak my adversary out by screaming, *"HIIIIIYAAAA!"* And then I run away—fast.

Even louder than my martial arts screech is the "crack!" of a gun when it fires. (This sound is partly from the bullet breaking the sound barrier.) The need for a quieter gun led U.S. agents during World War II to invent a barrel to fit over the end of a .22 pistol. Its purpose was to muffle the sound of the gun . . . so, it was one of the first silencers! This breakthrough led to different types of silencers being used today.

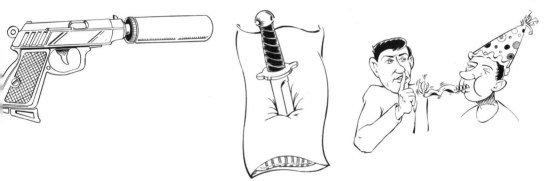

Although very useful, a silencer limits a gun's power and accuracy. To get around this problem, British agents in the 1970s came up with a "retro" weapon—a small, powerful crossbow that shot a short arrow (called a "bolt"). It could also shoot knife blades, which is pretty awesome!

Wait, I know what you're thinking: *"But there are all SORTS of silent weapons that spies could use, like daggers, tree twigs, and thermonuclear devices."* And you're right! But the problem with these weapons is that while they may be silent, the VICTIM will make noise while you're using them! For example, have you ever been stabbed with a thermonuclear device? I have, and it hurt so much I had to use my defensive screech: *"AAAAYIIIIIH!"*

In search of the most silent weapon of all, the U.S. Army developed a special poison dart gun.[3] Its dart was just slightly wider than a human hair. This made the dart almost impossible to detect, and the victim might not even notice he'd been shot until after he was dead.

THE TOUGHEST SPIES AROUND

Israel is a tiny country surrounded by nations that would like to destroy it. That means Israel's international spy agency, Mossad, stays busy! And Mossad's agents have been in so many dangerous operations, they are thought of as the toughest agents around.[4] There's even a joke about this:

A commander was told that there's a Mossad spy hiding on the other side of a sand dune.

"Ha!" the commander thought. "That Mossad agent is history!" And so he sent his entire platoon over the dune to get the agent.

Thirty minutes later, a lone soldier returned, nursing a knife wound.

"What happened?" sputtered his commander.

"It was a trap, sir," the soldier answered. "There were *two* of them."

---

3. The dart gun had a very silly name: "The Nondiscernible Bioinoculator."
4. Secrecy is another hallmark of Mossad. In fact, until 1996, no one even knew who the head of the agency was!

Of course, secret agents aren't usually out to hurt or kill people. It would be more convenient if enemy guards just had an "off" switch, but in my experience, these switches are really hard to locate. And despite what you see in spy movies, knocking someone out isn't easy. But if an agent *had* to knock a guard cold, he'd choose what's known as a *blackjack* (a.k.a. cosh or sap). This is a short club that has a heavy metal center, usually lead. That metal center is wrapped in leather, heavy cloth, or foam.

The idea is that as the blackjack hits someone on the head, the power of the hit will spread out a little. So the blackjack is less likely to break bones or cause bleeding than a hard wooden or metal club without padding. Even so, I think the safest way to dispatch your enemies is with a foam noodle. Sure, it will take more swings to get them to surrender, but safety first!

What other kinds of hidden weapons might enemy agents be using? To find out, I visited the website of the U.S. Transportation Security Administration (TSA). It's in charge of keeping air travel safe, and it has a handy list of hidden items that cannot be taken aboard an aircraft. Things like:

- Meat cleavers
- Spear guns
- Sabers (swords)
- Cattle prods
- Brass knuckles

- Nunchakus
- Throwing stars
- And my favorite: *snow globes* (really)

Yes, even snow globes can be used as weapons in the wrong hands. Best of all, the TSA forbids snow globes "even with documentation"!

Just now, I was wondering how many regular citizens are walking around out there with concealed weapons like snow globes or handguns. Let's see . . . it looks like over 400,000 people in Texas alone have permits to carry hidden guns. In that case, I'll have my spy agency equip me with a variety of devices. No, not firearms. Guns are for wussies! The genius of my hidden weapons items lays in the fact that no one would ever be suspicious of ANY of them!

And this brings me to the Worst Concealed Weapon Ever. Believe it or not, the KGB (Russia's old secret service agency) developed a weapon called the "rectal pistol." It was a small suppository (think of a gel tab someone might take for a headache) that an agent would hide up his . . . er, you know. Anyway, after retrieving the little tube, the single-shot canister would fire a 4.5 mm bullet if its barrel were rotated. (Imagine if it went off while the agent was hiding it!)

Speaking of Russian spies,[5] one was once caught in Germany with an interesting lipstick container. You see, it contained a bullet that could be shot out the container's "barrel"! Nicknamed the "Kiss of Death," the lipstick pistol was a good example of how spy gadgets can be built into ordinary-looking items.

Not to be outdone, the CIA came up with its own single-shot device: a tube of toothpaste nicknamed "the Stinger." This has always made me

5. For most of the 20th century, Russia was known as the Soviet Union (or Union of Soviet Socialist Republics or just USSR). This particular agent was a "Soviet." But to keep things simple, this book will always use the words "Russia" and "Russian."

wonder if a tired CIA agent ever checked into a hotel, then flossed and got ready to brush his teeth . . . and BANG!

There are also really high-tech weapons for self-defense. For starters, you already know what a Taser is. It's a great tool for when you need to take out an enemy spy or out-of-control lacrosse coach. But what if you're being attacked by a whole *squad* of lacrosse coaches?

What you need is the Taser Shockwave Barrier! (It's real.) The TSB fires two dozen electrified probes, all in the same direction. There's no escaping its shockwave barrier!

Plus, it gets you out of lacrosse practice.

Another thing I've always wanted is what's called an "Active Denial System" (ACD). (It's real.) The ACD fires a beam, and when it hits an enemy agent, he feels like his skin is burning. But it isn't! Yet it still makes the agent THINK his skin is on fire, and nobody can stay in the beam for more than a few seconds.

The ACD beam only penetrates $1/64$ of an inch into the skin. It's good that it doesn't go any deeper, because nothing stinks worse than an enemy agent engulfed in actual flames. The ACD does have some drawbacks. It's bulky, and if it's stormy outside, the raindrops will break up the beam.

That makes the enemy agent feel warm and refreshed, which probably isn't the response you're hoping for.

MAGIC AND UNMENTIONABLES!

Magicians have influenced many spy gadgets. For example, during World War II, a British magician named Jasper Maskelyne had an idea: Why not use fake tanks to trick the enemy? These props could be made from plywood. As long as they looked realistic to someone flying overhead, they would work!

This idea is still being used today. In fact, I was just looking at some photos of very realistic-looking Russian tanks. Their only drawback is that they're inflatable! All it would take is a nail in a tank's track, and *kaboom!* That tank would pop like a party balloon.

Famous magician/escape-artist Harry Houdini had a variety of blades and picks that he'd hide in the heels of his shoes. Houdini also had an oval container full of tools that he could hide in the back of his mouth. These could be used to pick the locks of the chains, chests, and rooms that he was locked in.

Inspired by Houdini, the CIA also invented a small toolkit of lock-picking devices. The tools were hidden in a four-inch capsule that looked like a giant pill. It was called the CIA

Escape and Evasion Rectal Suppository. (This makes me very uncomfortable.)

THE GADGET MASTER: CHARLES FRASER-SMITH

In the James Bond stories, the gadget master is known as "Q." This character was based on a real intelligence inventor named Charles Fraser-Smith. He was a British researcher who became famous for hiding gadgets, for example, concealing spy cameras in cigarette lighters.

During World War II, the Gadget Master came up with compasses hidden in coat buttons. To find them, you just unscrewed the top of the button. But the trick was, the compass-buttons unscrewed opposite from the usual way. Fraser-Smith's idea was that Germans were so logical, they would never guess that something might unscrew the wrong way! (And he was right.)

Another challenge for the Gadget Master was figuring out how to make British agents sneaking into France *seem* French. To do this, he made garlic-flavored chocolate for the spies to eat. (Don't all French people have garlic breath?)

As for the "Q" code name: During World War I, the British had sometimes disguised their warships as regular cargo ships.

These concealed destroyers were known as "Q-ships." After that, the letter Q came to signify any hidden meaning . . . or any wolf in sheep's clothing! So a Q-tricycle would be a beat-up looking average trike that is actually light, fast . . . and equipped with razor-sharp wheels!

In closing this chapter, let me say this: The tactics of spying have been the same throughout human history. Yet, spying technology keeps getting better and better, and it seems like a handy new techno-gadget is invented each week. My recommendation is for you to buy them ALL. (Then you can let *me* have your used night-vision goggles!)

ESPIONAGE
& Communication

Espionage is a secret activity that leaves no trace, so it's hard to get good information on it. Luckily, I'm here to answer your questions!

You might be wondering, "What's the best way for an espionage agent to gather information?"

There are a number of possibilities. Let's say you're into "industrial espionage." That means you've been hired to discover the secret products a business is developing. You could get started by hacking into the company's computers and pocket calculators. But here are two better ideas:

1. READ. Reading is the quickest and most reliable way to find out what's going on in the world. Following the news and "connecting the dots" is *very* important for intelligence work. In fact, experts say that 90 percent of what a spy needs to know is already public information. (The other 10 percent is in *this* book.)

In 2010, the FBI arrested ten undercover Russian spies. Not bad! But many spy experts shook their heads at how wasteful the Russians were. "Why not just have *one* Russian spy read an American paper every day?" an intelligence agent asked.

To prove this point, a CIA officer once hired five historians to write a report on the current state of the U.S. military. The historians had NO access to any top secret material. Instead, they just read newspapers, magazines, and books.

A couple of months later, the historians turned in their military report.[1] And when the CIA officer showed their report to other agents, the spies were astounded at how much good intelligence was in it. In fact, the historians' report was SO good that it was then classified as "secret" and hidden away . . . even though all the information in it had been public! That's why lots of librarians end up going into the spy business. (Really.) Librarians are curious, they know how to research, and they're good readers. These are all qualities a good spy should have.

2. TALK TO PEOPLE—IN PERSON! It's easy to fall into the habit of scanning aerial photographs, planting bugs, and staring at your iPhone. But professional spies agree that using *human* intelligence (a.k.a. HUMINT) is the best way to get the pulse of a situation.

---

1. Known as the Yale Report.

Think of it this way: a reporter might be the only other professional who is as interested in secrets as a spy is. And reporters often use "contacts" (people with inside information) to get their scoops. How do you get a contact? It can be complicated, but the key is to be trustworthy. This will be hard for you, because you're naturally deceptive. (You're a spy!) Your contacts have to believe that if they tell you something, you're not going to expose them. So don't!

HOT TIP!

With HUMINT, it can be tricky figuring out where to have a face-to-face meeting. A restaurant? Too romantic! A public park? Too obvious! I advise using building stairwells. They're not used much, they don't have bugs, and stairwells are also easy to escape from. (You just run down the stairs!)

DON'T KNOW WHOM TO TRUST? CHOOSE A WOMAN!

The most challenging part of HUMINT is knowing whom to trust. To help you with this, make a list of the most "suspicious" people you know. That is, people who you *suspect* might not be very trustworthy. (This could take a while.)

When you're done, look over the names. How many of your suspicious people are women? My bet is that it's less than half . . . and there might not be any! That's because most people think of women as being trustworthy. And that's one reason why many spymasters think that women make better spies than men.[2] Here are their arguments:

- 👁 Women have excellent social skills.
- 👁 Studies show that women are better at multitasking (doing more than one thing at the same time) than men. And if there's one thing a spy does, it's multitask!
- 👁 Women know more secrets than men, so they get more practice at learning secrets and then keeping them. Also, men are more boastful than women and are more likely to let something important slip out.
- 👁 Mothers know the importance of espionage in keeping track of their kids.
- 👁 Women might be more loyal than men.

Using HUMINT can take some interesting turns. About 2,200 years ago, the Roman Empire was at war with the African city of Carthage. During a truce, a group of Roman officers visited an enemy camp. They brought with them "slaves," who were actually other Roman officers in disguise.

Just to make sure that nobody from Carthage got suspicious, the Romans beat one of their slaves right in front of them! Naturally, nobody paid attention to the Roman slaves as they carefully memorized everything they could

---

2. This isn't to say that *no* men are trustworthy. *checking notes* Strike that. No men are trustworthy. Avoid them at all costs!

about the size and layout of the camp. After the meeting was over, the Romans went home. Then they came back and conquered the camp. (Oh, and the Romans won the war, too.)

SECRET COMMUNICATIONS

Once you start using HUMINT, you'll need to find ways to secretly communicate with your fellow spies and contacts. Yes, you could just send them a tweet from your Twitter account. But what if an enemy agent intercepts it? Do you have any idea of the horrible things they might do to that poor innocent little tweet?

Using other electronic communications might not be the answer either. In 2010, a suspect in a case regarding a bomb in Times Square was caught as soon as he used his cell phone. But if your phone or computer might be monitored, how can you send a message? There are countless options! For example, most spies learn how to leave rocks and sticks in a pattern that only the trained eye of another spy could possibly read. For example:

Speaking of "trained eyes," there was once a German spy with one glass eye. (Hey, that rhymes!) He had his eye custom made with a compartment in the back. There he would hide microfilm and other information. What an ingenious place to hide information—in his own skull!

There are lots of other non-electronic signals that you can use to communicate with others. A spy could go out in public scratching the back of her head. Sure, this LOOKS like an innocent natural gesture. But it turns out that hardly anyone ever actually scratches or rubs the back of their head! So it's a good "tip-off" signal for any friendly spies watching that the spy has information to share.

Something as simple as a baseball cap can also carry a hidden message. Is the cap's bill to the front? That might mean "Keep your distance; I'm being watched." Is the bill to the side? Perhaps the agent doesn't want to get a sunburned ear. You can see the possibilities. For example, another clothing technique could involve shoelaces. It's all in the way the shoelaces are laced!

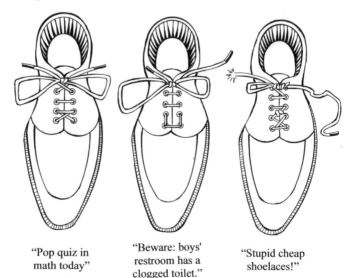

"Pop quiz in math today"

"Beware: boys' restroom has a clogged toilet."

"Stupid cheap shoelaces!"

DEAD DROPS

"Dead drops" are spots where a spy leaves cash, messages, or snacks for another spy. These dead drops might be indoors but are most commonly in outdoors locations. Just HAVING a good spot isn't good enough. The items left behind must still be camouflaged.

An example: American agents once set up an "audio dead drop" inside of a tree in a park. They placed a hidden microphone and a recording device completely out of view. So, a friendly spy or a diplomat would walk up to the tree, talk to it, and then walk off, trying not to look insane.

HE'S TALKING TO A TREE.

For spies operating in Russia, a Moscow park was the dead-drop spot. At an out-of-the-way location, they placed a custom-made hollow rock with a small computer inside. Spies would approach the rock and wirelessly download or upload information with their own handheld computers. This dead-drop rock system worked like a dream until the stone was discovered in 2006. Up until then, it was a great mix of 21st-century technology and the Stone Age!

★ *Secret Toilet Papers!* **German spies sometimes used a custom hollowed-out toilet paper holder for dead drops.**

Please do not confuse a "dead-drop spot" with a "drop-dead spot." These can be fatal. (That's a joke.) And speaking of fatal, spies have used the dead bodies of small animals to hide messages, memory chips, or film. Of course, the dead animal was first "stuffed" by a taxidermist, but the more disgusting it looked, the better. That's because even an enemy agent is unlikely to pick up a squished squirrel or rotten rat to see what's inside of it!

However, agents found that one problem with hiding secrets inside of dead animals was that cats sometimes ran off with the bodies! To foil the felines, agents began sprinkling their "host carcasses" with hot chili sauce. The cats (who may have been agents themselves) left the dead animals alone after that.

While we're in the animal kingdom, agents agree that if you need to do some dead drops, you should get a dog. That's because a dog gives you endless excuses to leave the house and then go on odd little trips where you can easily make dead drops and pick up dog dookie. Wait—I guess the dog dookie isn't that helpful, is it?

Or you could follow the example of Chinese spies a thousand years ago. They would write a secret message, seal it in wax, and then swallow it. Within 24 hours, they'd be dropping some secret dookie themselves!

HOW TO DEAD DROP!

Imagine that you're ready to set up your own dead drop. You're going to leave something important (like a doughnut) for your contact at an indoor location. (Better yet, imagine that you are leaving a doughnut for yourself!) For this dead drop, you'll need a plastic container with a lid (like the ones that hold leftovers in the fridge) and a few strips of Velcro.

Attach one strip of Velcro to the bottom of the plastic container. Now attach the other strip to the underside of a table or desk that is your dead-drop spot. Pop the doughnut into the container and put the lid on. Turn the container upside-down and stick it up to the other side of the Velcro strip! (If the container doesn't hold, just use more Velcro.)

When your contact comes along, he doesn't have to worry about ripping the Velcro apart and making a noise. All he has to do is quietly pop the lid and let the doughnut fall into his hand. Ta-dah!

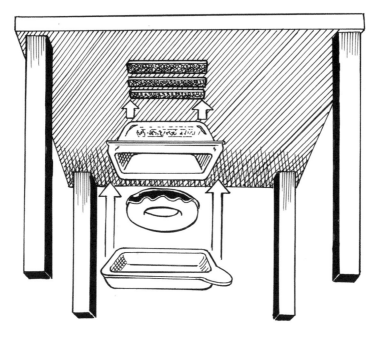

What else? Well, you've probably seen those "Hide-a-Key" containers before. These little containers with a magnet can be hidden or stuck to small, out-of-the-way spots. (Agents call these "clam dead drops.") And if you have a pond, lake, or stream nearby, consider getting a waterproof pouch that you can hide underwater for a later pickup. Make sure to anchor the pouch under a rock, though. Otherwise, your secrets could float downstream and wash up ashore!

BRUSH CONTACTS

The time will come when you need to actually pass information to a contact in person. As this is more dangerous than a dead drop, you need to be careful, and practice how to do a "brush contact." Here's how:

While walking down a sidewalk or school hallway, you see one of your contacts. If he isn't already expecting to receive something from you, give one of the signals that the two of you already have. This signal should be something subtle, like rubbing your nose or doing the chicken dance.

Now, as you approach each other, put the item you're going to pass in the palm of your left hand. Don't look at each other. As you pass on the right, secretly slip the item into your contact's left hand. This is a thing of beauty when it works, but it looks kind of dumb if one of you drops the item, sort of like a bad baton handoff on a relay team.

SMUGGLING

As you're out on missions, you may need to carry some things with you that you don't want others to know about. One way to disguise the items is with an old, outdated hardcover book. Encyclopedias from the 20th century are perfect for this. Your best choice is to go to the library and find out when and where they sell old books that are no longer considered useful. These books usually cost less than a dollar; look for a thick old hardcover and buy it.

When you get home, put on some heavy work gloves and get an Exacto knife. Be careful, an Exacto blade is sharp—*razor* sharp. (That's because it IS a razor.) Better yet, get an adult to use the knife. Now, take a piece of cardboard and slip it into the book about twenty pages before the *end*. (Trust me.)

Now turn to pages 20–21, near the front. Using a pencil, outline a rectangle that is about an inch inside the edges of page 21. Have your adult helper cut deeply along these lines with the Exacto knife. It might take a bit of cutting to get all the way through to the cardboard at the back side of the book, so carefully push down. Once you've cut a hollow rectangle into your book, trim the edges, recycle the cuttings, and you're in business! You can hide any dastardly item you want in the book, like deviled ham, a digital camera, or digital ham.

Now, why did I have you go to the library to get this book? Because in the history of humankind, nobody has ever looked suspicious carrying a library book!

That book cover makes the perfect cover. Best of all, your book makes the perfect item for dead drops as well. Just go to the library, make sure your contact sees you, and then leave the book on a shelf. Handoff complete!

Another great way to leave a message for someone is with a newspaper. Take a paper and turn to the crossword puzzle. Write your message, one letter per square, across the puzzle. Then fill in the rest of the squares with random letters. Refold the newspaper and hand it off with a brush contact or leave it at a dead-drop spot.

A FINAL WARNING ON TRUST

In 1917, there was a revolution in Russia. A new Communist government was set up, and many Russians who feared for their lives fled the country.

Assuming that anyone who had left was an enemy to the "new" Russia, the Communists created an agency nicknamed "the Trust." Its mission was to persuade the Russians who had run away to **RETURN HOME**. Using a variety of methods, the Trust did entice a number of former Russians to do just that.

After all, if you can't trust the Trust, whom can you trust? Nobody! Once these Russian emigrants were back, they were usually imprisoned. (Or worse.)

DISHONESTY—
It's the Best Spy Policy

Anyone becoming a professional spy knows she's going to have to break some rules. By rules, I mean *laws*. Think about it! The CIA has about 5,000 full-time spies. That means it has 5,000 *lawbreakers*.

Like me, I'm sure you are very disturbed by this. But here's one way to look at it: laws in your country are broken every day by spies from *other* nations. So it wouldn't be fair if your country's spies didn't do the same thing back![1]

Maybe calling a spy a "criminal" is too harsh. How about if I describe what spies do as "cheating"? That still sounds judgmental? There must be a better word! Let's see, I could use *deceive, trick, scam, dupe, hoodwink, double-cross, gull, con, rook, finagle, bamboozle, flimflam, sucker, hornswoggle, pull a fast one* . . . hmmm, on second thought, "cheating" is just fine.

---

1. I know, that's a really lame argument. And it's also the one that spies use.

Anyway, every country has a small army of professional cheaters who are good at sneaking around to get secret information. What kinds of tricks do these rascals use? I'm glad you asked!

TRICKS OF THE TRADE

1. Look Dumb!

Yes, highly trained spies try to look stupid. That is, spies really *don't* want to look alert, smart, or in any way genius-like. Let me put it this way: no one thinks a nitwit can come up with a clever plan. And no spy wants to be thought of as clever by the people he's trying to spy on. (This is why I often drool; it lulls people into a false sense of security when I'm around.) After all, which of these people are you going to be more suspicious of?

WHICH IS A SPY?

CRAFTY
PROFESSIONAL

HARMLESS
IDIOT?

2. Stick and Move!

Another key to trickery is to simply *keep moving!* This is especially useful in social situations. Let's say you sneak into a party to gather information. A suspicious woman comes over to you.

"Who are you?" she asks.

Thinking quickly, you say, "I'm Joe's boss."

"And who is Joe?" the woman continues.

"My employee," you answer. Good one! But you're not going to be able to keep this up much longer, so get moving.

"And there he is now!" you add, walking briskly out of the room with a smile.

3. Go to the Right Schools!

Before World War I, British intelligence agents could take classes in the "Technique of Being Innocent," the "Will to Kill," the "Technique of Lying," and something called "Dr. McWhirter's Butchery Class." (Yikes!)

Check with your local schools and libraries to see if they have any courses that teach spy skills. If not, ask any neighborhood kids wearing trench coats if they know of any good classes. (Those kids are so suspicious, they have to know *something*.)

4. Cheap Tricks Are Better Than Genius Plans!

Don't think that because you're a spy, your plans have to be masterpieces. Sometimes a simple plan is the best plan.

For instance, if you need to get someone away from his desk for a moment, tell him that you think you saw his car get hit in the parking lot. Actually, it's even better if you can get someone *else* (like building security) to pass the word along.

DEAR WARLORD: YOU'RE DUMB!

Over 2,000 years ago, a Chinese peasant named Liu Ji worked his way up to being a rebel leader and, eventually, emperor. Not bad! One of Liu Ji's strategies was sending messengers to enemy leaders. The messengers had simple messages, like "You suck!" and "You're a moron!" And these would often enrage the enemy leaders to do stupid things . . . like leading their troops into ambushes!

5. Get a Kid to Do Your Dirty Work!

Adults naturally think that all kids are innocent. And kids think that any kid younger than them is also *dumber* than them. This makes children the perfect accomplices, but only if you can keep them from sticking gum in each other's hair. The Russians used this to their advantage (see p. 72), and you can too!

6. Be a Smooth Operator!

British spy Richard Tomlinson once explained the challenges he had to deal with during his training. For one exercise, Tomlinson and his fellow students had to approach a perfect stranger and find out the person's name, job, birth date, and passport number.

Tomlinson pretended he was the captain of a yacht and invited two women for a cruise the next day. Since they were going to sail from England to France, Tomlinson told his "passengers" that he'd need just a *little* information from them: their names, jobs, birth dates, and passport numbers!

Tomlinson was smart by pretending to be a ship's captain. As soon as someone sees you as an expert, you become an authority figure. You see, people don't question authority figures like professors, police officers, or the authors of spy books.

7. Distract a Target by Getting Him to Talk About Something He's Interested In!

People LOVE to talk about themselves . . . so, find out what your target's interests are and find a way to work it into the conversation. Let's say that you know your target likes to can pickles. At some point, work that into the conversation.

"Canning pickles is one of my favorite hobbies. What's that? You like to can pickles too?"

Now is the perfect time to use flattery:

"I'm sure your pickles are way picklier than mine."

And finally, make some small mistake that gives your target a chance to show off his or her knowledge:

"As you know, pickles come from cucumbers harvested by fishing boats—Huh? They grow in gardens? Wow, it's lucky that I'm talking to you."

And *now* you're ready to smoothly pick your person's mind.

"Have you ever noticed that pickles are shaped like nuclear missiles? I wonder how many nuclear missiles YOUR country has?"

8. Copy the Con Men!

Like spies, professional con men are good at tricking people
(a.k.a. "suckers"). Unlike spies, con men then take their
money! And a study on these criminals found that con men
often follow these two rules:

- 👁 Appeal to a person's greed. Once you know what the
  target wants, you can easily manipulate him.
- 👁 Try to get your target to do something dishonest. If you
  can get him to do something wrong, it will be harder for
  him to ask for help once he's been conned, scammed,
  tricked, suckered, or otherwise ripped off!

9. How Many Times Do I have to Tell You?
Use Magic!

In the 1950s, the CIA hired professional magician John
Mulholland to write a manual of trickery and deception
for its agents. When you think about it, this makes perfect
sense. Magicians misdirect an audience's attention, often
while making things mysteriously disappear . . . and this is
pretty similar to a lot of intelligence jobs!

There probably isn't a spy out there who wouldn't benefit
from practicing a magician's skills. (Even if I can't think of a
practical use for cutting someone in half!)

10. Be Creative!

As you're presented with new challenges, keep on exercising your brain to figure out your best approach. For example, during the Revolutionary War, the American spymaster with the code name of Agent 711 was *extremely* creative. You might know Agent 711 as someone named "George Washington."

THOSE SPYMASTERS WERE MONEY

Benjamin Franklin ran spy networks in France during the American Revolution. That means that the men on the U.S. dollar bill *and* the hundred-dollar bill were both spymasters!

Washington was so terrific at his job that after the war, the head of the British intelligence operations said, "Washington did not outfight the British, he simply out-spied us." Naturally, George Washington knew that British spies were keeping an eye on his forces. But he didn't let that worry him! Instead, Washington made his officers and men spread out their camps along the sides of the roads. This sometimes put them miles away from each other, and the soldiers grumbled. But there was a reason for it.

Imagine that it's morning. A British spy in costume is walking along the road, when he sees some American soldiers making breakfast. The spy makes a mental note of where they are and then keeps traveling. Over the course of the next five miles, the spy sees groups of American soldiers making their breakfasts the entire way!

The spy then duly reports that Washington's army seems to cover five miles—and that made it *seem* like the army was MUCH larger than it actually was! How George must have laughed and laughed.

EAVESDROPPING!

As all spies know, a "bug" is a hidden mini-microphone. And kids love them!

Kids know better than anyone how fun it is to be sneaky. For example, in 1946, a group of Russian schoolchildren gave the people at the U.S. embassy in Moscow a gift. How sweet! It was a carved wooden wall decoration of the Great Seal of the United States.

This gift from the Russian children hung on a wall in the ambassador's home for the next six years. And then a U.S. security team discovered that the carving had a microphone in it. It turned out that Russian agents had been listening in on the ambassador all that time. Those little brats gave us a bug! What made the bug especially hard to detect was that it had no power source and it didn't send radio signals. That's not bad technology for way back then!

Here's what I love about this story: to solve the bug problem once and for all, the United States decided to have a *new* Moscow embassy built in 1968. The idea was to carefully watch the Russian workers so they wouldn't try any funny stuff. The problem was the Russians constructed the walls away from the building site, and then trucked them in to Moscow. And even worse, the Russians even mixed electronic bugs into the concrete mix for the building.

The result? By the time the new embassy was done, it had so many listening devices, it was just a gigantic radio broadcaster! The United States had to spend $40 million more just to start over. Dang it!

Of course, you don't need technology to eavesdrop. Sometimes you can just be standing right there. Take Mary Elizabeth Bowser. She was a slave owned by Jefferson Davis, the president of the Confederacy during the Civil War. By keeping quiet, Mary was able to gather all sorts of

ONCE BUGGED, TWICE SHY

Because the Russians were so aggressive about bugging, U.S. agents sometimes overreacted. During a high-level meeting in Vienna, Austria, two American agents wanted to sweep a meeting room of any bugs. Investigating the room above the meeting area, the agents found a big brass object in the floor. They didn't know what it was, but the thing was suspiciously mysterious!

The two agents worked all night with a toolkit to remove the device. When they unscrewed a rod from inside of it, the brass object finally came free! But as they went downstairs, the agents realized they had made a *big* mistake. The meeting room couldn't be used anymore because the huge antique chandelier in its ceiling had just crashed to the floor and broken into smithereens.

Oops!

intelligence (especially while serving dinner!), because Davis and his guests assumed she was illiterate.

Burn on them! Mary was born in 1839 as a slave in Virginia. But after being freed by her owners, Mary attended school and received a good education. Because she was both highly intelligent and a good actress, Mary was enlisted as a spy for the Union.

In her role as a spy, Mary pretended to be Ellen Bond, a slow-witted servant who worked at the Confederate White House. And she was treated as if she were invisible! So while doing housework, Mary would read the letters and strategies that were left out in the president's studio. While serving meals, she would listen in on conversations about military strategies and troop movements.

Best of all, Mary had a nearly photographic memory, so she could repeat what she had read and heard word for word!

As the war went on, Jefferson Davis knew there was a leak *somewhere* in his office or home, but he didn't discover the source until it was too late. It is sad but understandable that after the war was over, the U.S. government destroyed all records relating to its spies in the South, including Mary. This was done to protect them from revenge. And Mary knew a few things about secrets herself, as she then disappeared entirely from the historical record!

EAVESDROPPING TIP!

If you have two cell phones, you can listen in on almost anything. First, set one of the phones to "silent." Then go to the area where you want to eavesdrop. Find a place where you can "plant" the silenced phone. This should be a spot where it won't be noticed but *will* be out in the open.

Now call the silenced phone and answer it to establish a connection. Set the silenced phone to "hands-free" or "loudspeaker" and leave the room!

Take the phone you'll be listening in on to another room. If it has a "mute" feature, use it, so you can hear through the other cell phone but any noise you make is blocked. If you can't do this, just be quiet!

Even though her later life remains a mystery, Mary Elizabeth Bowser was one of the most important espionage agents of the Civil War. And remember that she did her best work just by keeping her ears open!

By now, you understand the need for keeping your ears peeled. Sure, it's painful, but that's part of an agent's job. And now for an inspirational tale of surveillance:

Imagine that you're an agent stationed in the tropics. Your Spymaster thinks that enemy forces are using a certain jungle trail, so you have to bug the trail! To make sure the bug isn't found, you have to hide it in something that will not be a tempting place for the enemy to look. What do you choose?

If you worked for the CIA, you would have picked tiger poop! During the Vietnam War, spy bugs were placed inside real-looking brown clumps. The bugs inside of the fake poop did just what they were supposed to do: they revealed enemy troop movements. (And the enemy troops didn't move the fake poop because it looked like an enemy *bowel* movement.)

Okay, let me share a spy tale with a little more class. When Madeleine Albright was the U.S. Secretary of State (1997–2001), she had her own particular style. For example, Albright wore jewelry pins that reflected her mood. If things were going well, her pins were butterflies and balloons. Not so good? A spider pin or maybe a snake accessory.

At one point while Albright held office, a sweep of the State Department offices discovered some bugs. Who had planted these listening devices? The Russians! So can you guess what kind of pin Albright wore to her next meeting with the Russians? Yep, a bright bug.

"They got the message," Albright said.

Of course, there have been many times in history when a nation didn't realize that its enemy was getting its message. For example, at the start of World War I, the Russian army just used regular radio broadcasts to give regular commands. There was no jamming, no codes, no tricks—just orders! Because radios were so new in 1914 that the Russians hadn't considered that someone ELSE might be listening in.

As a result of this mistake, the Germans wiped out an entire Russian army at the city of Tannenberg. Double-oops!

BUGS WITH BUGS?

One of the CIA's greatest listening devices was the "insectothopter." This was a remote-controlled fake dragonfly equipped with a tiny motor that a watchmaker made. The flying spy would buzz around and set listening devices outside of windows. The insectothopter worked great, too. But it was so small that if it flew into a breeze it was thrown off course and lost.

Or was it really lost?

SURVEILLANCE

Admit it: you've been secretly observing people for years. How else could you pounce on the last piece of pizza *every* time?

In spy agencies, this is called "surveillance," and I'm glad you've already had some practice. A good spy like you can secretly observe an individual, a group, a company, or even an entire nation without anyone knowing it. In fact, I've been secretly watching the country of Lichtenstein since 2007. (Luckily, it's not very big.)

And now, I have a special treat: this is the only surveillance story involving diaper rash that you'll read in your lifetime!

In the 1950s, the CIA worked with airplane makers to develop a spy plane called the U-2. It was designed to take high-quality photos from altitudes over 70,000 feet in the air. Back when it was built, that was higher than Russian jets or even missiles could fly. In fact, 70,000 feet up is where outer space begins!

The U-2 flew so high and on such long missions that its pilots had to wear space suits with built-in diapers. As one spy plane pilot said, "I learned the hard way . . . that you can get diaper rash from Gatorade"!

In 1962, U.S. spy planes took photos of new missile-launching sites in Cuba. But since Cuba didn't have the ability to make missiles, that meant that Cuba's ally—Russia—had to be the supplier.

President John F. Kennedy called in a Russian diplomat named Georgi Bolshakov to explain. Bolshakov was outraged! He acted insulted and denied that there were *any* missiles of *any* kind in Cuba.

So, the Russian was shown the spy plane photos. "And what do you think *those* are?" he was asked. Bolshakov hesitated. Then he smiled and said, "Baseball fields, perhaps?"

Ha! President Kennedy was too polite to do it, but right then he could have shouted, "That's the *second*-worst excuse of all time!" (The worst excuse of all time comes a little later in this chapter.)

Thanks to spy satellites, surveillance has only gotten easier since. The first U.S. spy satellite was launched into orbit in 1961. But think about it: while those early spy satellites could *take* pictures of the earth below, there was no easy way for us to *get* those photos!

Back then, the spy satellite had to eject its film into a container called a "camera pod," and then the pod had to be ejected from the satellite. It would plummet down to the earth, and then the pod had to be retrieved, sometimes from the other side of the planet! Finally, the film had to be developed, and by then, a LOT of time could have passed. In fact, in 1967, there was a conflict known as the Six-Day War—and that war was already finished before satellite photos of it started to come in!

Since the 1970s, digital technology has made it possible for satellites to "beam" photographs and other information back to Earth. If you've used Google Earth, you know there are now swarms of satellites circling the planet and beaming pictures down to it. That's a lot more convenient, and it means that today, *anyone* could be under observation at *any* time.

But even though spy satellites can spot an individual person, they still can't track that last piece of pizza. So, keep your eyes open!

FREEZE-FRAME!

Since you don't have clearance to the best spy satellites, *always carry a camera*. And practice being sneaky with it!

- 👁 Change the settings on your camera so that it will not automatically flash or make sounds. Nothing is worse than setting up the perfect stealth shot and then giving yourself away with a loud *beeep*!

- 👁 Practice taking pictures while holding the camera at your waist. This means you won't be looking through the camera's viewfinder or screen. Experiment with different wrist angles, and remember that most digital cameras require you to push a button halfway down to focus before snapping the picture.

- 👁 Once you are decent at "shooting from the hip," try doing it while covering the camera with a long-sleeved T-shirt, sweater, or coat. (The idea here is to cover the *camera* but not the lens!)

- 👁 Fire away with the camera while *not* looking right at your target.

👁 If you think you've been spotted, try turning or moving away from the target while still snapping pictures.

👁 If you're still worried about being spotted, get a "fake key chain car-lock spy camera." This small device looks just like a car key lock, but it has a camera built into it. Assuming there are some cars near the thing you want to take a picture of, you just aim and push the button. The device makes a sound as if it were locking a car, but instead, it's shooting video or taking pictures![1]

Sometimes it's not the camera that prevents you from getting a photo—it's *you*. In cases where you need to disappear, plant a camera in a concealed spot where nobody would expect it!

CLICK

1. Do you know why key chains are such a great invention? They let you lose *all* your keys at the same time!

SPIES ARE LOOKING AT YOUR ONLINE PHOTOS!

Innocent bystanders can gather important intelligence without realizing it. Imagine a tourist in Paris. He is trying to get a shot of his Aunt Ruby by the Eiffel Tower . . . Just as he snaps the photo, foreign agents *steal* it. No, not the picture—they steal the Eiffel Tower! But just as the criminals commit their very unrealistic crime—**click**—the tourist photographs *them*.

Regular people really *do* take pictures of top secret things all the time. Professional spies call these kinds of photos "Aunt Minnies" because someone's aunt (or other relative) is often in the picture.

And that's why intelligence agents right now are online and looking through people's Facebook photos. (Seriously.) This job used to be a lot more difficult. During World War II, U.S. agents were sent out on missions to antique stores. There, they would look through photo albums, trying to find good Aunt Minnies. (Seriously!)

AUNT RUBY IN AN AUNT MINNY

TALKING TRASH

But surveillance isn't all glamorous hip-shooting and cuckoo clocks. Sometimes you're going to have to roll up your sleeves and get dirty! Going through a subject's trash is a great way to find evidence of what she's been up to. But don't actually TAKE the person's trash away. That would be stealing! (It really is.) However, most experts agree that it's legal to go through any garbage that's been set out on the sidewalk or in a dumpster.

Of course, it looks a little suspicious if you're seen going through someone's garbage bags. In 1991, a police officer spotted two men doing just that in Houston, Texas. An investigation showed the men were searching the trash of a technology company bigwig. And more investigation showed that the men worked for the French government. *Sacré bleu!*

This led the French Embassy to release *the worst spying excuse of all time.*

Yes, the trash collectors were employees of the French government. But, no, they weren't spying! Instead, the men were "collecting grass cuttings to use as fertilizer in the French embassy's garden."

They should have used that *excuse* in the garden instead, because it was pure bull manure!

GARBAGE TIME

When double-agent Aldrich Ames came under suspicion, FBI agents went through all of his trash every week and then *put it all back the way it was* for nearly a full year!

Big candy companies spy on each other all the time. During one of Nestlé's spy campaigns against the Mars company (see p. 288), agents went dumpster diving outside the Mars headquarters for months. To make sure nobody noticed the missing garbage bags, the agents *replaced* them with different bags of trash.

Then the Nestlé agents had to sort through the bags they had taken. Inside were coffee grounds, shredded documents covered in food, and even underwear. (*Blech!*) The spies had to be tough because their job was to take those soggy pieces of shredded documents and patch them back together!

Now let's set our surveillance sights a little higher. Did you know that there are a number of small model helicopters and planes that can be fitted with cameras? Of these devices, my favorite is one that falls off of maple trees.

Or at least the device *looks* like it fell off a maple tree. Students at the University of Maryland invented what they call the "world's smallest controllable single-winged rotocraft." This micro-vehicle looks like a maple seed and isn't much bigger. If you've ever seen a maple seed fall, you know that it has a unique spiral flight due to the "wing" attached to the seed. This camera-fitted rotocraft uses that same movement to take off from the ground and hover. Or you can just hold it in your hand and toss it into the air!

COMINGS AND GOINGS: THE STAKEOUT!

Keeping track of who is where when can be tricky. Let's say you need to know when a particular person drives away from a certain place. You could stakeout her location , but that might take five minutes . . . or longer!

If you have a cheap wristwatch, simply wrap it in duct tape. Then slyly stick it underneath one of the car's tires that is closest to the curb. At some point, the person will drive off, running over the watch. Later, you can come back and grab it, and the time the hands stopped on the watch is the time your person drove away.

Oops, you didn't use a digital watch, did you? That won't work for this technique! And neither will large timepieces that might be spotted by the driver.

BE A FOLLOWER!

If you're ever assigned to "put a tail" on someone, don't sweat it. The more nervous you are as you follow your target, the more likely it is you'll get spotted. And remember, it's not the end of the world if you get discovered. Unless, that is, a spy delivers the plans for the Ultimate Death

Machine to some evil genius. (In that case, it *is* the end of the world, and thanks for nothing!)

As you develop your tailing skills, remember: if you're tracking someone who *might* be suspicious, you don't want to constantly be behind him. Instead, get in front of him! Whether from the front or behind, try to get into the walking rhythm of your target. Concentrate on his movements and move in harmony with him . . . but be careful. If you get *too* tuned in to his movements, the two of you may break into a song-and-dance number!

You'll probably have some idea of where your person is headed, so walk ahead and then stop at a "choke point"—for example, a spot where lots of people are going in and out of a building—and see where your target is. Now stay alert!

◉ Don't make sudden movements as you work. If you're diving into doorways, everyone will notice you.

◉ Don't move your whole head when tracking your target. From a distance, he'll be able to see this. Instead, use just your eyes to look *near* your target, but avoid making eye contact with him. If you can, follow your target's progress by watching his reflection in windows.

◉ Most importantly, *never make eye contact* with your target! As soon as you do this, you might as well give up. Because even if the person doesn't recognize you, he will probably remember you if he sees you again! (This is especially true if your target is one of your parents.)

That's one reason why following a target is best done with at least one other person. If you have a partner, a hands-free cell phone will work great for communication. (And if one person gets spotted by the target, the other can take over entirely.)

With your surveillance team, your goal is to put a "floating box" around your target. With two people, this means that one person is in front of the target and one is behind. But with three people, you can also have a person across the street who is keeping an eye on things.

LAST THING

When secretly following someone, do not make the mistake of the four-year-old kid I was just playing hide-and-seek with. He believed that if he couldn't see *me*, then I couldn't see *him*.

So to hide, he just closed his eyes.

How dare that gnome challenge me with his primitive skills? I found him *every* time. *Yes!* (I'd high-five you right now, but it's apparently impossible.) The tyke reminded me of the people who walk around with their hoodies pulled over their heads. You just know that lots of them are putting the rest of the world in an "out of sight, out of mind" category.

If you're trying to conceal your identity, don't pull up your hoody. It just makes you look **MORE** suspicious. And I guess that's a good reminder that it's time for me to talk about disguises!

DISGUISES,
Alibis & Covers

When it comes to concealing your identity, nothing works better than using a rubber cow.

Don't believe me? During World War II, British agents came up with a collapsible rubber cow disguise. Just like in cartoons, it had room for one person to be the head and two front legs, and another agent would be the cow's back legs and butt. And just like in cartoons, I'm sure this led to some interesting arguments!

The idea was that two spies would have the cow outfit and then parachute at night into a pasture with cows in it. Genius! The spies would conceal their parachutes and then hide in the cow outfit in case anyone came looking for them.

But even if you have a cow costume, how are you ever going to disguise yourself? You don't even know what *you* look like. Of course, neither do I! Here's what I mean: if you've listened to your voice on a recording, you might not think it sounds like you—even though it does! That's because it's hard to get a good perspective on YOURSELF. You're too close to the subject.

So while you THINK you know what you look like, you really don't. And this makes disguising yourself difficult! To get around this problem, ask four people to make a short list of your most visible, obvious features. In other words, if you were standing in a crowd, what would someone notice about you? These are NOT value judgments. So don't take them personally. Also, we're not doing a fashion makeover here. We're just trying to define what fashion of person you already are!

Now, look at the feedback you've gotten and see what you can do to disguise yourself!

FEEDBACK	DISGUISE
You walk funny.	Walk seriously.
You have long hair.	Buy a skullcap, hairnet, or visit the barber.
You are short.	Wear platform shoes and long pants.
You are tall.	Look, do I have to figure out *everything*?
You mope and wear a lot of black clothing.	Smile and wear Hawaiian shirts and Californian pants.
You are thin.	Wear thick padded clothing.
You are thick and padded.	Wear thin clothing.
You wear glasses.	Take the glasses off. (Good luck!)
You have a big Adam's apple.	Wear a fake neck-beard.
You are elderly.	Carry a child-safety seat. (Tell people it's for you.)
You are young.	Squint and tell "the whippersnappers" to stop muttering.

You should realize by now that spies can be ANYWHERE. They are professionals at blending in. This especially applies to spy-assassins. Recently, there was a case in Dubai where 11 disguised assassins walked into a luxury hotel. And after they arrived, the spies "removed" a terrorist leader. What kinds of awesome disguises did *these* murderous pros use? Hats, glasses, and fake beards. That's it!

These items were easy for the agents to add or subtract from their disguises—and that's the key! An important part of disguising yourself is being able to make quick changes. For example, you've probably heard of reversible jackets. Let me suggest taking that idea one step further. I have two words for you: *reversible underwear.* One quick trip to the bathroom and *ta-dah*! Of course, no one else will notice the change, but you'll act differently. (Maybe.) And people will DEFINITELY think you're a different person if you add or remove a bad hair weave, straw hat, gold tooth, or even a cast for a broken arm.

PORTRAIT OF AN ASSASSIN

To make quick changes, it's important to carry a change of clothes in a backpack or duffel bag. But (and this is important) have a DIFFERENT backpack or duffel bag inside of the one you're carrying. That way, when you duck into a restroom to put on an overcoat, fake goatee, and a homburg (that's a hat), you won't come out still carrying the same old Adidas bag.

By using these simple props, you should be able to fake your way into all sorts of situations!

Just as important as your appearance is your body language. If you're American, it's likely that people from other countries will notice that you put your hands in your pockets, slouch, lean against walls, and chew gum. (Seriously.) So don't do ANY of those things when you're out on a mission! Instead, try standing up straight and using your hands a lot when you talk.

It's also possible to change the way you walk. Try putting a pebble in one shoe and a slice of Swiss cheese (cheddar also works) in the other. As your feet go through strange new sensations, you will find yourself walking with a new disguised gait.

NOT-SO QUICK CHANGES!

★ Grow a beard.

★ Cut your beard.

★ Let your hair grow out.

★ Cut your hair.

★ Put a scarf around your throat.

★ Cut your thro—*hey, wait a minute!*

As for your voice, it's possible to disguise it during phone conversations from public phones or borrowed cells. But don't try to fake an accent! You will just sound like yourself trying to fake an accent.

Instead, take a pen or pencil and put it between your teeth. Then speak carefully. This will change your speech enough to fool whoever is on the other line, even if it's the greatest spy of all time. And the amazing thing is—OUCH!

Sorry, I just had a sharp pain. You see, I suffer from *ninjavitis.* This is a condition where ninja assassins make frequent attempts on your life. As annoying as these murderous pests can be, ninjas can also teach us a few things about concealment. You see, the word "ninja" comes from the Japanese word *ninjitsu*—the art of making oneself invisible. Based on the movies I've watched, the first way to go about this is to wear a black coverall with a hoody and a face mask. You may scoff, but as far as I can see, once you put on this getup, you can walk on tightropes and hang from trees by your toes for hours on end.

DO YOU SUFFER FROM NINJAVITIS?

Going black has its advantages, especially at night. But when you go out in the day, "go gray." That means blending in with your surroundings so that you can disappear in a crowd of two. Do most people your size and age wear T-shirts and sneakers? Then do the same thing and watch how invisible you become. On the other hand, maybe top hats and cummerbunds are the "cool threads" in your part of the world. If so, start packing! Because it's time to move to a place where people wear T-shirts and sneakers.

If you're a man, it's much easier to dress "down" than to dress up. In other words, if you're following someone downtown, wearing a suit is a good call. And if your target goes to a soccer match, you can always take off your necktie and drape your jacket over your arm. Then buy your ticket, and you'll still fit in with the crowd.

The following goes without saying, so I'll write it: If you're disguising yourself, be sure to remove anything distinctive that you usually wear, like jewelry, suspenders, or tattoos. Don't wear white shoes, and don't wear clothes that contrast with each other, like a dark shirt with a light jacket. Try to dress generically (which means that there's nothing "flashy" about you). Just try to fit in and act normally. In a library? Carry a book. In an animal feed store? Carry a pig.

We can learn a valuable lesson about concealment from King Alfred of Britain. After his kingdom was invaded by

Vikings, Alfred dressed up as a minstrel (a wandering music maker) and then went to the Viking camp to entertain the troops. Since wandering entertainers were common, Alfred was able to get into the camp and play a harp near the tent where the Viking commanders were making their plans. Talk about getting some good intelligence!

Later, when Alfred led his army into battle, not only did he win, but he also earned a cool nickname: "King Alfred the Great." (This is far better than his other nickname: "King Alfred the Harpist.")

When spies like King Alfred go into enemy territory, they have to be extra careful. That's why British spies landing on beaches in Asia during World War II wore special boots that left behind barefoot-shaped imprints in the sand.

OOPS, WRONG BOOTS.

Speaking of shoes, if you ever want to use your shoes as a special tool for walking in a whole different manner, put them on the wrong feet. As your feet go through strange new sensations, you will find yourself walking with a new disguised gait. Trust me, it works wonders!

An unusual disguise was used in the Civil War by a spy pretending to be a black male slave. The slave was actually a woman named Emma Edmonds . . . a *white* woman. Working for the Union, Ms. Edmonds cut her hair, wore a wig, and dyed her skin darker . . . and incredibly, the disguise worked!

If Emma Edmonds could pull off that disguise, then it's entirely possible that you have seen a disguised agent before. You just didn't know it at the time! The agent may even have been wearing a mask—and not some cheesy Halloween-type mask either. The CIA makes the best masks in the world. They allow the skin beneath the mask to breathe and appear totally natural.

FOR WHEN YOU'RE SPYING ON GIBBONS

In the late 1970s, make-up master John Chambers did the costumes for the *Planet of the Apes* movie. After the movie came out, CIA officials were so impressed, they hired Chambers to do disguises for government agents!

HIDING THINGS!

Whether you're at home or on the road, as a spy you're going to need to learn how to disguise and hide your secret stuff. Let's go over some tips:

1. Do NOT hide things under the bed, under the mattress, in your pillow, or in your shoes. Do you know why? Because that's where everyone always looks!

2. Some people have had success hiding valuables in the freezer. This is an especially good place to keep any ice cubes you have that are collector's items.

3. This is a really cool tip: Experts often put valuables in a large ziplock freezer bag. But they don't put the bag in the freezer. Instead, they use safety pins to fasten the bag to the INSIDE of clothes that are hanging in the closet. No one would ever think to check there! This technique also works with curtains or drapes as long as the bag is are pinned so that it's not visible from inside or outside.

ALIBIS & COVERS

While having a complicated disguise is not necessary to
be a spy, having an ALIBI is. Your alibi is your false reason
for being where you are. The key is to have a good—but
not *too* good—alibi. And make sure to have the right props
and "pocket litter" to back up your identity. ("Pocket litter"
is what spies call the stuff in your pockets that make your
story real.)

For instance, "I'm here doing a survey" is a good alibi, but
it's worthless if you don't have a smart phone or a clipboard
with some paper. And if you ask, "Have you seen this dog?
I'm looking for her!" you should be able to show a photo of a
dog—AND you should be carrying a leash.

CRYPTONYM: AN AGENT'S FAKE NAME

If you're a really smooth operator, you won't even need to
explain your alibi. For example, Robert Baden-Powell (who
founded the World Scout Movement in 1907, which included
the Boy Scouts) was a British agent who loved adventure
and enjoyed acting. This led to escapades like the time he
once drenched his clothes in brandy and then wandered
out on a military dock in Germany to spy on a ship. Baden-
Powell was immediately arrested. Oops! But since he
reeked of alcohol and was acting like a drunkard, he was
sent on his way—having gotten the information he wanted!

On a mission to Croatia in the late 1800s, Baden-Powell's job was to learn about the strength of the forts in the region. So he took a sketchbook and a butterfly net and set out. Baden-Powell then disguised his sketches of fort layouts *within* his sketches of butterfly wings!

ACTIVITY!

You can easily do something similar on a computer. Just take your secret document or information. Now "select" all the text and copy it into a PowerPoint document. Select and change the color of the text so that it matches the background. And *now*, copy and paste a big picture over the whole thing. When you send it to another agent, all that person has to do is delete the picture and then highlight the text behind it to reveal your message!

COVER: A FALSE IDENTITY

On the other hand, you might be trying to conceal your *identity*. That means you need something stronger than an alibi—you need a COVER. A cover is your false identity or job. It's the same thing as an alibi but just more complicated. Picking the right cover is important! It has to be something that you can fake doing reasonably well. For example, Rita Elliott was a Russian spy. Her cover? Well, she worked in a circus. Good cover! This gave Rita a chance to travel all over without looking suspicious. But Rita's job at the circus was as a tightrope walker. This could be a very BAD cover if she hadn't been skilled at her work!

Some covers aren't especially dangerous though. For example, the National Rifle Association is against any form of gun control. So the NRA hired a woman named Mary Lou Sapone to pose as someone who was FOR gun control. Sapone then joined important gun-control groups and became a part of their leadership boards. Sure, Sapone was a spy, but she probably wasn't that worried about getting caught. After all, what were the gun-control people going to do—shoot her?

One of my favorite covers is that of an agent named Wolfgang Lotz. After World War II, a number of Nazis fled to the Egyptian city of Cairo. Israel was concerned that among these Nazis were weapons specialists and rocket scientists that might help the Egyptian military.

Israel needed someone on the inside. And it had just the man! Wolfgang Lotz may have been an Israeli, but he was born in Germany, had a German-sounding name, and most important, looked VERY German. To top things off, Lotz was a super-confident "party guy-spy" in the James Bond mold. His nickname was "the Champagne Spy."

Lotz moved to Cairo. His cover was as a wealthy horse breeder. It was in this role that the rumor got around that Lotz used to be in the German military. Pretty soon, the Champagne Spy was hanging out with a bunch of Nazis!

Lotz sent information back to Israel by means of a radio transmitter hidden in the heel of his riding boots. Nice! His best adventure might have been when he went spying at an Egyptian rocket base near the Suez Canal. The Israelis thought this launch site was a "dummy" designed to confuse their military.

But to make sure, Lotz and his wife pretended to go fishing. The two of them drove right toward the rocket base and were arrested. Lotz apologized and explained that it was an honest mistake. Even so, the arresting officers took Lotz right ONTO the rocket base, which was obviously NOT fake! (In other words, there were rockets there.)

Lotz (who was in handcuffs) asked the base commander to call an Egyptian general that he knew. The general asked to speak to Lotz and said, "Do you want to rot in jail, or will you pay up with a bottle of champagne?"

Lotz went with the champagne. Aren't you paying attention? He was the Champagne Spy! Although his cover worked well on that occasion, Lotz was arrested by the Egyptian police in 1965. He was jailed for three years, and then sent back to Israel in a prisoner exchange.

Wow, what a story. Now let me close this chapter with the simplest, most effective disguise that I know of: the finger mustache!

ANIMAL SPIES

As we know, the key for any spy is not to look suspicious. And what's less suspicious than an animal? Well, okay, a plant is less suspicious, but it's really hard to get a birch tree or even a small shrub to follow orders. And that's why critters, beasts, and varmints have been used many, many times in the world of espionage.

What—you think animals haven't won or lost wars before? Ha! About 2,500 years ago, spies from Persia noted that their Egyptian rivals loved cats. So when Persia went to war with Egypt in 525 BCE, the Persians had a secret weapon: cats! As the Persian soldiers marched forward, they held kitty cats.

Since the Egyptians thought cats were the coolest animals of all time, they wouldn't shoot any arrows at the Persians. And it was hard to win a battle back then without shooting arrows. The Egyptians lost!

This shows that the Egyptians were wrong about two things: how to win a war and what the coolest animal of all time is. You see, the Egyptians SHOULD have focused their attention on . . .

DOGS!

Almost all people like and trust dogs. That's why they can be the ideal helpers for a spy! For example, a French agent used a dog as an assistant during World War II. The agent was in a part of Southeast Asia that was under Japanese control. The agent knew that if he were caught sending a secret message to the French, it would mean certain death.

So he shaved his dog!

Then the spy took a pen loaded with indelible (permanent) ink and wrote an intelligence report on the dog's skin. After that, all he had to do was wait for the dog's hair to grow back. As soon as Fido was hairy again, the agent just took the dog for a LONG walk and presented the canine to a French spymaster. One shave-job later and—*voila*—secret message received! This message is now famous as the Dog Skin Report.[1]

Not only can Spot carry spy messages, he can also spot spies! For instance, in 1985, the Russians suspected that their own spy, Oleg Gordievsky, was a double agent for the British. (That's because Gordievsky WAS a double agent for the British.)

Knowing he was being watched, Gordievsky left his Moscow apartment to go out for a jog—and kept on running! By bus and train, Gordievsky made it almost to Russia's border with Finland. There, he hid in the trunk of a car being driven by a female British diplomat. The woman drove up to the border, showed the KGB her papers, and got ready to drive through—until a Russian guard dog began sniffing her car's trunk. That darned dog was going to ruin Gordievsky's escape!

Thinking quickly, the woman distracted the dog with a meat sandwich. And her incredible plan worked! This led to one of the most famous rules in the history of spying: *"A guard dog would rather eat baloney than sniff Gordievsky."*

---

1. Really. The original idea for it goes back to the ancient Greeks (see p. 168).

Speaking of dog smells, one of the strangest products the CIA ever made was a liquid that would attract male dogs and make them howl. The idea was to spray the substance[2] on the doorsteps of suspected enemy spies at night. That way, howling dogs would annoy the agents, and they wouldn't get a good night's sleep!

This might lead to the agents being tired and forgetful the next day. Maybe they would do something dumb, like leave their secret documents at the ice cream shop. (Hey, you never know!)

LET SPYING DOGS LIE!

If you'd like to enlist your dog to confuse enemy agents, try this: Get or borrow a pair of small walkie-talkies. Using Velcro strips, attach one of them to your dog's collar. Turn on the walkie-talkie and tie a handkerchief around the dog's neck to conceal it.

Have a fellow agent take the other walkie-talkie. This agent needs to stay nearby. Now, as you walk your dog, approach enemy agents. If no enemy agents are around, just go up to anybody who doesn't seem too scary. Act casual when your dog makes a statement like, "We will break up your spy network and destroy you."

Because spies love disguises, sometimes THEY like to be the dog. Seriously! In the 1970s, the CIA came up with a way for

---

2. Called "Dogs in Heat."

an agent to sneak around in a country without being detected. First, one agent would enter the country with a St. Bernard dog. These colossal hounds can be the size of a small pony!

Then if a spy needed to get somewhere unobserved, he would check in with the St. Bernard's owner. There, the spy would put on a St. Bernard dog suit and crawl into a portable kennel. The spy would also bring a small tape player and begin playing the sounds a St. Bernard makes: snoring, slobbering, and snoring.

The kennel would then be transported to a veterinarian so the "dog" could get a checkup. Once inside the vet's office, the spy would get out of the kennel, take off the dog suit, and leave. But he probably wouldn't bring the tape of snoring and slobbering as it's unlikely that it would be helpful with his next assignment.

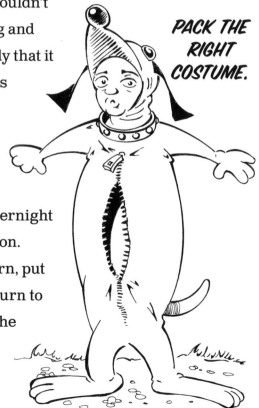

PACK THE RIGHT COSTUME.

If anyone was observing all this, the fake dog could be left overnight at the vet's for observation. Then the spy could return, put the suit back on, and return to the dog-owner's house the next day!

SEA LIONS AND DOLPHINS!

The elite U.S. Navy unit named SEALs (Sea, Air, and Land team) is made up of humans. But the Navy also has a Marine Mammal Program in San Diego that trains California sea lions and bottlenose dolphins. I love dolphins—they're so cute! But what could these delightful mammals be doing for the military?

Apparently, the dolphins can go "get" enemy divers! One Navy animal trainer said, "We train them to either pull the mouthpiece from the diver's mouth or push him to the surface." Apparently, dolphins have been armed with syringes loaded with pressurized gas. And if this syringe were poked into a human diver, it would cause the person to blow up. *Blech!*

I guess dolphins aren't so cute anymore.

Along with sea lions, dolphins are both very intelligent and **WAY** faster in the water than even the best human swimmers. Navy sea lions are trained to carry cuffs in their mouths that are attached to long ropes. If they find a suspicious swimmer, they can clamp the cuff around the person's leg and the intruder is then reeled in like a big spy fish.

And it turns out that even the most skilled divers usually never even see the sea lion before being clamped and hauled to the surface.

And the sea lion will do all this for some fish! Amazing.

Current plans are for dolphins to patrol the waters off U.S. bases to watch out for terrorist swimmers. If the dolphin on patrol sees an intruder, it activates a powerful strobe light to alert its handlers. The light would then float to the surface, and guards would race to the spot in speedboats.

But these militarized sea mammals are also trained to do more peaceful things. For example, people aboard ships drop things overboard ALL the time.

"Careful with that top secret canister."

"Yeah, yeah. Listen, I've got it—"

splash

"Top secret canister overboard!"

This is where having a trained sea lion comes in handy. Not only can a marine mammal locate and retrieve objects lost overboard, it can also look for underwater mines. (Seriously, the animals are trained to do that.)

What if a sea lion or dolphin accidentally triggers the mine and gets blown up? To prevent loss of life, the U.S. Navy developed underwater robots that check for mines.

Called Unmanned Underwater Vehicles (UUV), four of these water robots were put to the test by the Navy in the waters off Virginia. Oops! All four of the UUVs were lost at sea. So who did the Navy send to find them? The same dolphins and sea lions the robots were supposed to replace!

★ At the end of the 20th century, the CIA built a realistic robot catfish called "Charlie." To this day, no one knows what Charlie's secret mission was, but some experts think he was designed to collect water samples close to chemical or nuclear plants.

WHEN HAMSTERS INFILTRATE
YOUR HOME

If you have a hamster cage or aquarium in your house, you might be able to pull off this amusing spy trick. See if there's a spot where you can mount a digital camera behind the cage or aquarium. The idea is that you're going to take a photo (or series of photos) from that spot, using the camera's timer. And because the photo will show the room seemingly from *inside* the animals' habitat, it will look like the hamster or guppy took the picture!

Assuming you have your camera mount ready and the timer settings correct, simply wait until you hear people coming into the room. Then set the camera and stand back so you don't block the shot. Be sure to have the flash turned off and the camera sound on "mute" so that others don't notice when it snaps the photo. If you can only take one shot at a time with your automatic settings, you might have to do this a few times to get the shots you want, but patience is an important part of spy work. (If you're not that patient, just use a video camera instead and start recording.)

Once you have your shots, the fun part is the way you reveal the footage! If you have photos, print them out and put them in a manila envelope. Then add a note written by the hamster or guppies, maybe something along the lines of *"I've been spying on you for months. If you don't want me to tell the authorities about your actions, start giving me better hamster (or guppy) chow. And plenty of it!"*

Then mail the letter to your house, or just shove it through your home's mail slot, and try to keep a straight face!

CATS!

As I noted earlier, cats can be good additions to an espionage plot. After all, cats are known and loved for their intelligence and grace. And they're also known for their cunning, paranoia, and murderous impulses.

Wait a minute, cats are **TOTALLY** untrustworthy!

No matter. Back in the 1960s, the CIA recruited cats to be part of their spy program. The felines were going to take part in Operation Acoustic Kitty. (No, I am not making this up.) The idea was that a cat would be trained to follow certain commands. Then it would be outfitted with a little microphone and antenna. When ready, the cat would slink around during a cocktail party and listen in on people's top secret discussions about nuclear missiles and cheese-on-a-toothpick.

Perhaps you can see the problem with Operation Acoustic Kitty. Yep, it's the "cat would be trained" part! It turns out that in the history of mankind, no cat has ever been trained to do *anything*. So if the Acoustic Kitty was released at a party, it was totally unreliable. The program ended when a CIA agent released a spy cat in a park to go eavesdrop on some people. The cat ignored orders and strolled off into the street, where it was hit by a car!

That was the end of Operation Acoustic Kitty.

VOCABULARY

"Walking the cat" is what CIA agents do when an operation goes wrong. The idea is to go back to its beginning, and then walk through the plan again to spot where it went off target.

PARACHUTING BEARS?

Could parachute-wearing bears have sniffed out Osama bin Laden? I mean, a bear's sense of smell is much more powerful than a bloodhound's. So why not use bears to sniff out the terrorist?

The Defense Department gets suggestions from the public all the time. Sometimes citizens write in with good ideas. Sometimes the ideas are decent. And sometimes the ideas are insane.

Take this idea about terrorist-hunting bears. It was sent to the Defense Department and written about in a *Stars and Stripes* article: "Trained bears with GPS and day/night cameras around their necks might be able to hunt down the scent of Osama bin Laden, even in and through any caves and tunnels! Parachute some bears into areas [that bin Laden] might be. Attempt to train [the] bears to take off parachutes after landing, or use parachutes that self-destruct after landing."

Well, that sounds simple enough! Ooh, and here's a citizen question for the Defense Department:

"So do you have any top secret information you would to like to tell me? I am doing a project for my senior economics class, and was just wondering . . . email me back."

BIRDS!

Back in the primitive days of the 20th century, there were no cell phones. (Astounding!) So animals were sometimes used to carry important messages. And that's why British and American forces used hundreds of thousands of messenger pigeons in both the First and Second World Wars. This could be dangerous for the birds. Once, when an American battalion began getting shelled by their OWN forces miles away, they used a pigeon to take word back to the nimrods shooting at them to lay off. The pigeon was named Cher Ami. And that brave little pigeon got his message through despite losing an eye AND a leg on the flight.

Cher Ami was treated like a hero after his mission, but not all of our feathered agents are so lucky. For example, a pigeon in India was recently captured and held under armed guard. Why? It was suspected of being a spy for India's archenemy, Pakistan!

Indians grew suspicious when they spotted a pigeon with a ring around its foot. And once it was captured, Indian pigeon keepers insisted that the bird was totally suspicious. This was partly because of the Pakistani phone number and address stamped on its body in red ink—and also because the experts said that Pakistani pigeons look totally different from Indian ones!

Sadly, the pigeon couldn't tell its story. After all, you can't expect a pigeon to sing like a canary. But if the pigeon *is* a foreign agent, it's not going to be returned. This means that Pakistan gave India the bird![3]

_____

3. Did you see that? *Two* jokes in *one* little paragraph!

WORMS!

You probably already know that silk comes from silkworms. (These are actually moth caterpillars, but whatever.) And these silkworms spin silk out of their butts! That's a pretty good trick. I'd like to see a sheep try that with wool! (Actually, I wouldn't.)

Anyway, there was once a day when most of the world didn't know what silk was, much less where it came from. But then about 1,500 years ago, the ruler of the Byzantine Empire (in southeastern Europe and Turkey) sent spies to China with hollow walking sticks. Their mission was to pretend to be messengers looking for a trade agreement. Actually, they were supposed to be finding and stashing moth eggs in their walking sticks to smuggle home!

It's not like silkworms are the ONLY worms that have been involved in espionage. During World War I, British spies faced a problem: How could they read maps at night without attracting enemy fire? The solution was to read by the light of glowworms! Sure, the Brits had to strain their eyes by the glowworms' pale light, but that still beats getting a howitzer shell up the nose.

SNEAKING,
Following & Escaping!

I got in trouble the first time I went out on a mission. It was just myself and an agent named [*name deleted*]. As the two of us made dead drops, staked out enemy agents, and stopped for a quick shopping trip (I had a coupon for pickles!), I'd tweet our precise location. (I did this so my mother would know that her favorite child was safe.)

But when [*name deleted*] found out what I was doing, she was **NOT** amused. She took away my iPhone, broke my Twitter account, and confiscated my pickle jar.

Luckily, I had another coupon!

Anyway, my theory now is that spies should be like hikers. That's because when hikers go into the wilderness, their goal is to **LEAVE NO TRACE** that they were there. Nothing but boot prints—and maybe some buried poop. As a spy, you want to follow that example! (Except for the part about the poop.)

In addition to leaving no trace, remember that escaping the scene of your espionage doesn't just mean that you get away *today*. It also means that you don't get caught tomorrow or the next day either.

So develop your powers of observation and cunning! Let's say that you've been tipped off about a top secret item that's in a room. Don't just go waltzing in to take it! As you approach the room's door, carefully look at the handle *before* opening it. Why? It's possible that someone has sprinkled a small amount of baby powder on the door handle to see if any intruders tried to enter. (I do this all the time at my house.)

★ **The KGB invented a "spy dust" that could be revealed using infrared lights. It was sprinkled on the doorknobs to important rooms. Then guards or officers would shine infrared lights on people's hands to see if anyone had been sneaking around.**

It's also common for paranoid people (like me!) to place a small piece of clear tape on the door and frame. That way, if an agent returns to a room and the door tape is broken, she knows someone has been in there!

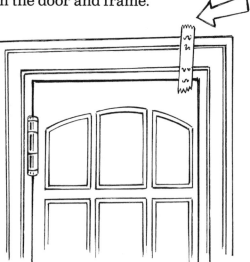

Solution: If you use the door handle,

either avoid touching the powder or sprinkle new powder on it as you exit. As for the tape, note *exactly* where it is. Open the door. Then when you leave the room, do your best to replace the tape with a new piece.[1]

Now you can enter the room safely, especially if the door is unlocked. But when you push the handle down or turn the knob, KEEP it pushed down or turned until you're through the door. Then gently close it and slowly let the handle of the knob latch. Nice and quiet!

If the door is locked, just use a key. No key? Pick the lock, already! (You'll find lock-picking instructions on p. 783 of this book.) Right, so now you're walking in, and you feel the small rug in front of the door give way slightly beneath your feet. Aha!

Rolling up strips of modeling clay and putting them under a rug is yet another way of seeing if an intruder has come into

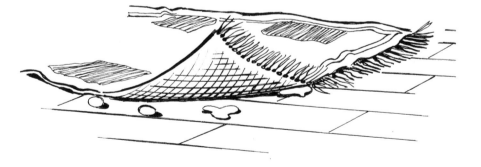

---

1. Instead of using tape, people have been known to wet a long hair and stick it to the door frame. I've always found this disgusting! So if you see a hairy door, I recommend you leave.

a room. If you return and find that the strips of clay have been squished, it's a giveaway!

Solution: When you leave, carefully lift the rug, reroll any clay strips you might have squished, and step around the rug on your way out.

Finally you approach the desk. You can see that what you're looking for is underneath a tray of marbles. Why marbles? Because whoever set up the tray took a digital photo of exactly where the marbles are!

Solution: Take a picture of the marbles yourself. After getting what you came for, rearrange the marbles according to the picture.

Now you're almost there. After moving the tray to the side, you're ready to accomplish your act of espionage. It looks like that box of Cap'n Crunch is waiting for you! Uh-oh . . . you need a bowl and some milk!

Solution: Get a bowl and some milk.

In the event that you found something less tasty, like perhaps a secret file, you need to get it and get out. But the problem with going out the door you came in is that you can't see through it! What if a big security guard is approaching from the other side? To detect the presence of approaching meanies, lean down and gently place your front teeth on the door handle. The best way to detect vibrations is to touch metal, and few things are as sensitive to vibrations as your teeth! Is it silly for a spy to seemingly be eating a door handle? Yes. Does this work? Yes!

SNEAKING QUIETLY

So let's say that you're trying to move around without making a sound. Yes, that rhymes, but that's not important now. What *is* important is that you're not carrying any pocket change or keys. They jingle! And turn off your cell phone, too.

And for goodness sakes, BE QUIET. So don't wear wooden clogs. And avoid corduroy clothing because the fabric rubs against itself and makes noise. Some spies think wool is the quietest fabric. Other spies think NO fabric is the quietest fabric of all. (For those agents, the best disguise is no disguise . . . and no clothing, either!)

Before doing any professional sneaking, you may want to practice sneaking up on animals. That's because an animal has senses that are far more sensitive than a human. So, if you can sneak up on a cat, you can *definitely* sneak up on an enemy agent.

I'm practicing this right now with our tomcat, Captain Sugarmittens. Ha! This furball is sleeping so deeply, he doesn't realize that I'm reaching out right now to grab his tail—

THERE'S THAT DARN CAT!

AAAH, GET HIM OFF MY FACE!!!!

Oh, you are *bad*, Captain Sugarmittens. You just gave your daddy a third nostril! But at least I learned a valuable lesson. When indoors, you can avoid making floorboards and old stairs creak by stepping as close to the wall as possible. That's how Captain Sugarmittens caught me just now.

So THAT'S the reason why spies and cats both skulk! I mean, have you ever seen a cat go through a doorway? It stays close to the edge of the door and peers around the corner with one eye. If the coast is clear, the cat goes through but still sticks by the wall.

Cats also like to stay close to things they can hide behind, like sofas, chairs, and larger, fatter cats. Since these cats need the exercise, let's go OUTSIDE for the rest of this training. Now, if you ever find yourself sneaking around in woods like these, try to avoid stepping on the dry twigs—
    crunch
Who was that? Mom? Timmy?
    crunch
Captain Sugarmittens?

Wait, it's me! And if I'm trying to creep up on someone, I still haven't given myself away yet. With dry forest floors, don't just plod along with a *crunch, crunch, crunch*. Instead, try to take irregular steps. That means you might *crunch*,

crunch, pause, slide your foot, stop for 20 seconds, *crunch*, etc. There are all sorts of animals out in the forest, and you might be able to fool someone listening into thinking that you're one of them!

BEING TAILED

Do you think you're being followed? Maybe you are! If you've noticed someone near you twice in one day, it could just be a coincidence. But if you're out and about, and you see your suspect 17 times, that's too coincidental to be a coincidence! My guess? You're under surveillance! Now what? Try these tactics:

1. If you constantly look behind you, your tail will know that he's been spotted. So if you're on foot in a city, glance at shop windows to look behind you without looking behind you. Pop into a store, glance at a rack of bibs, and then pop back out. This gives you a chance to survey the whole street in both directions before setting off again.

2. Try turning a corner and quickly putting on or taking off a hat or jacket. Or turn a corner and run fast for a few steps. Or turn a corner and duck into a shop or doorway.

   I guess what I'm saying here is that you need to turn a corner.

3. If you spot the person who you think is following you, turn around sharply and start walking in the opposite direction. As soon as your tail's back is to you, start running! Then turn around and see what your suspect is doing. (Note: be careful, as you're now sprinting in one direction and looking in another.)

4. The BEST way to spot a tail is to have a team (or at least one other person) working with you. The idea is that your team tails you while looking for anyone else who looks like they're tailing you too. You can station members of your team at certain "choke-points" where flow is restricted. These choke points might be narrow sidewalks or hallways, entrances or exits, or spots where people are actually choking on food that they should have chewed more before trying to swallow.

VOCABULARY

Dry cleaning: The process of using a team to spot a tail.

Here's something you already know: People who get on escalators face in the direction they're traveling . . . and almost never turn around! So if you get on an escalator, go about halfway up and then quickly turn around. Did someone behind you quickly look away? They're busted! And if a team of people is trailing you, there is probably someone in **FRONT** of you as well. Watch the people getting off; does anyone turn to check if you're there or loiter at the top of the escalator? If so, they're busted, too!

Before you have to make any fast getaways in a car, I strongly recommend that you carry with you a dummy that CIA agents call a Jack-in-the-Box (JIB). Some JIBs are inflatable. Others are like simple robots that just show the top half of a human body and have heads that automatically turn back and forth as if looking around. Either way, from behind the car, the JIB looks like a real person. So if you're being followed, you stop, set up the dummy and leave it in the car seat as you secretly exit from the other side.

EXIT ROUTES

As you've been learning, making a getaway requires advance planning. This is true if you're at home lounging in your pajamas and enjoying educational cartoons. Then suddenly, you see enemy agents closing in!

This is the time when your organization pays off. You sprint toward the TV, open the bottom cabinet doors, and access the escape tunnel you put in months ago!

Or perhaps you're spending quality time at the playground. From atop the slide, you spot a group of enemy mothers pushing strollers and closing in! You quickly slide down the slide and run to the swings.

Getting a nearby kid to push you, you soar through the air, and leap into the sandbox. From there, you access the escape tunnel you put in months ago. Crawling through it, you finally emerge through its trapdoor, which happens to be right back at the . . . slide.

Uh-oh.

TRAVEL TIPS!

When staying at a hotel, stay away from the ground floor. That makes it too easy for enemy agents to sneak into your room. It will also make it harder for them to throw things like stun grenades or fattening snacks through your window.

Speaking of which, have you ever been in a hotel room that had a shared balcony with the room next door? For obvious reasons, you don't want that kind of room. Also, avoid any room that is across from another room with higher windows. (This makes it too easy to spy on you!)

Okay, so now you're headed to your room. A bellhop stops you in the hallway and asks what room number you're in. What do you do? If you've been paying attention, you give him a FAKE room number. That punk could be a spy! After all, bellhops are naturally suspicious . . . what possible job could possibly involve *bells* and *jumping*?

Continuing, you take the elevator to the floor ABOVE your actual floor. Then you take the stairs down. Why? A spy never goes right to his destination.

As you get settled in, you check your luggage for the doorstop you packed. These little wedges are handy to insert beneath the door when you're in a room. That way, even if someone has a key to your room, he can't get in!

Okay, you're safe and sound—wait, you left your fattening snacks in the lobby! Rats.

There's no sense in complaining about it, though. After all, you're lucky to be alive . . . unlike the agent in the next chapter.

OPERATION MINCEMEAT:
Based on a False Story

O peration Mincemeat is famous for making a hero out of a dead man. That is, the man was dead BEFORE the operation began . . . and *then* he became a hero. Operation Mincemeat is also famous as the most successful intelligence operation of World War II. And it started like this: In 1943, a Spanish fisherman spotted a decomposed corpse floating in the water. *Yuck!* The body was handcuffed to a briefcase. *Interesting!*

After the dead man was fished out of the water, he was identified as a British officer named Major William Martin. Spanish authorities opened his briefcase and found that it contained a military envelope. *Really interesting!* Meanwhile, British officials began sending a blizzard of messages asking for the return of the dead major's briefcase, and ESPECIALLY any envelope inside it.

A German spy caught word of the hubbub. He got his hands on the envelope and snuck its contents out without breaking the seal. What the spy found was a secret Allied plan to invade Europe from Greece!

This amazing spy discovery made it all the way to Adolf Hitler's desk. But the Germans had to be careful! They had to make sure that the Brits wouldn't think that anyone knew their secret plan!

So the spy returned the secret plan to the envelope and put it in the briefcase. The Spanish returned the briefcase and Major Martin's dead body to the British. And the Germans started sending major troop reinforcements to Greece and Sardinia to fight the coming invasion.

That's when the British must have been tempted to yell, "SUCK-ERRRS!" You see, British spies had dumped that dead man off the coast of Spain on purpose. Why? Let me back up a little and explain.

In 1937, intelligence agent (and future James Bond inventor) Ian Fleming read a detective story. It was about a dead man who was found carrying secret papers that turned out to be fake. When World War II began, Fleming remembered the detective story and it gave him the idea for Operation Mincemeat. The goal was to save thousands of soldiers' lives by faking an Allied invasion at one spot but then REALLY invading at another!

★ *How Much?* One of Ian Fleming's spying co-workers once said, "Fleming is charming to be with, but would sell his own grandmother."

Following this daring plan, British agents threw the dead man overboard off of Spain. He was actually a Welshman named Glyndwr Michael and had nothing to do with spying or the war. His uniform, fake ID, and briefcase had all been carefully prepared and planted on him by British agents. And after the body was found, the frantic British attempts to get the briefcase back were all staged. The Germans had to be fooled into *thinking* that the British had been fooled!

But it was the Germans that were duped in one of the biggest deceptions in all history. Because when the REAL Allied invasion happened in Italy, the German troops in Greece weren't any help. More than 3,000 ships carrying an invasion force of 160,000 Allied soldiers landed successfully, and they had a dead man to thank for it.

Now that you know about the trickery of Operation Mincemeat, you're ready to learn more about something called *misinformation*!

MISINFORMATION

Edward Lansdale was a U.S. agent who came up with an interesting way to confuse opponents: Lansdale would publicly THANK enemy leaders for their help! This would lead to conversations like this:

Enemy Soldier: How did you help that American spy?

Enemy Leader: I didn't!

Soldier: Then why did the Americans send a singing telegram just now, thanking you for your assistance?

Leader: He is just doing that to make you suspicious of me!

Soldier: So you DIDN'T help him?

Leader: No! Of course not!

Soldier: Yet I have never known a singing telegram to be wrong . . .

That Edward Lansdale was a tricky one! In fact, ALL spies are tricky. A man named Peter Ustinov wrote a story about how tricky a spy's life is. In it, a small country named Concordia is caught in a power struggle between the United States and Russia. To survive, Concordia needs to be crafty!

So, to play the two countries against each other, Concordia's spymaster tells the American ambassador that the Russians have broken the secret U.S. code.

"We know they know our code," the American says. "We only give them things we want them to know."

Concordia's spymaster is stunned! He walks to the Russian Embassy and tells their ambassador, "The Americans know you know their code."

The Russian answers, "We have known for some time that the Americans knew we knew their code. We have acted accordingly—by *pretending* to be fooled."

Amazing! The spymaster then returns to the American Embassy and tells them, "The Russians know you know they know you know."

"What?" the American ambassador says in surprise. "Are you sure?"

But in the crazy world of spymasters, there is no way to tell if the American ambassador is only PRETENDING to be surprised!

This kind of tricky deception can be called *misinformation*. This is a lie intended to trick a person into thinking that *fiction* is *fact*. And once the mistake has been made, the result can be disastrous.

MISINFORMATION: THE SAMURAI WAY!

For example, the Taira and Minamoto clans were two warring factions in medieval Japan. During a battle, the Taira sent a small group of their best samurai fighters to the front line. These fighters challenged the Minamoto to do likewise. The proposal was that only the elite samurai would battle to the death. In this way, fewer people would be fighting and lives could be saved!

The Minamoto agreed to this idea, and they watched with great interest as their handpicked samurai fought for the clan's honor. What the Minamoto DIDN'T see was the army of Taira warriors creeping up behind them. Or maybe the Minamoto samurai DID see them at the last second as their heads were cut off their bodies by those misinforming, sneaky Taira warriors!

Here's another case where a little misinformation had colossal consequences. About 200 years ago, Napoléon Bonaparte ruled France. But he wanted more power! To help make himself look good and his opponents look bad, Napoléon had his spies forge a document supposedly written by the ruler of Russia, Peter the Great.

In it, the fake "Peter" said that he wanted to conquer the world. Naturally, the world was very concerned about this!

So to protect everyone from the big, bad Russian, Napoléon kindly stepped in to save the day. (Then Napoléon tried to conquer the world himself.)

Adolf Hitler used misinformation when he created an excuse to invade Poland. In 1939, German spies faked a Polish attack on a German radio station near the Poland/Germany border. "Operation Canned Goods" involved German intelligence agents dressed in Polish uniforms entering the radio station. The fake Poles took over the radio microphone, gave a short speech encouraging Poland to attack Germany, fired a few shots, and left.

Even though the whole thing was bogus, it gave Germany the excuse it needed to invade Poland. On September 1,

1939, German troops crossed the border, and World War II was underway.

VOCABULARY

Confusion agent: A spy who *doesn't* spy. Instead, he spreads misinformation to confuse enemy agents.

Misinformation should be almost impossible today. I mean, fact-checking on the Internet is so simple! Yet, somehow, spreading misinformation is more popular than ever. All a person or group has to do is lie, lie, lie. And then lie some more! The key is to repeat the misinformation over and over in a variety of ways. For example, have you ever seen anonymous email chain letters? These are either "funny" or spouting some kind of misinformation. (Or both.) And between misinforming emails, blogs, television shows, and even text messages, once these lies are out, there is always *someone* who believes them.

Technology also gives governments a wide range of choices for making themselves look good and their enemies look bad. This can be as simple as hiring thousands of people to go into Internet chat rooms and write "[Country X] is good!" China is famous for doing this, and something tells me that China is not alone.

Of course, people can always turn to trustworthy experts and websites for the truth. But it's amazing how few people do this! As the leader of the fact-checking site Snopes.com said, "When you're looking at truth versus gossip, truth doesn't stand a chance."

Wow, that's kind of a sad way to end a chapter. But I know just the thing to cheer you up: sabotage and assassinations!

SABOTAGE
& Assassination?

Look, I'm not writing about antisocial topics because *I'm* antisocial. I'm VERY social! I even go out of my way to have tea and crumpets with little old ladies.

Wait, what *is* a crumpet, anyway? Dang, my own misinformation just tripped me up.

Back to business. It's important that you learn about topics like *sabotage* (SAB-uh-taj) so that you can ~~commit mayhem~~ stop enemy agents from committing mayhem. As you know, sabotage means to destroy or damage things for spy-like reasons. But sabotage can't just be vandalism. Have you ever heard of a spy painting graffiti? Of course not! Spies rely on cunning, so their sabotage has to be intelligent and sneaky.

For example, during World War II, American agents snuck explosives into piles of coal that were going to be burned in German factories. Why weren't these bombs quickly discovered? Because they were disguised as pieces of *coal.* Sneaky!

Oh, and in 1942, American scientists came up with an explosive that looked like wheat flour. They nicknamed it "Aunt Jemima," and it could be used to make pancakes or biscuits. The pancakes were even *edible.* But if you attached the proper detonator, those pancakes would blow up the kitchen.

The Germans also committed a clever form of sabotage against the Allies: they printed trainloads of fake British money. Then they tried to sabotage the British economy by flooding markets with the counterfeits. The idea didn't really work, but it gets points for originality.

Of course, sabotage is frowned upon everywhere. But maybe if you commit very SMALL acts of sabotage, no one will notice. For instance, imagine your dad's making tuna casserole. *Blech!* Slip into the kitchen and give the oven a nudge to "broil" for ten minutes. Then slip in again and turn it back down. That should take care of the problem.

> **Dad:** Sorry, everyone, but the casserole's burnt! Reckon we'll have to get pizza.
>
> **You:** Rats. Well, if you insist.

While you may become frustrated with law enforcement officials who prevent bigger acts of sabotage, let's not sell these do-gooders short. I mean, it's too bad nobody waved off the French secret service back in 1985. That's when the environmental group Greenpeace was protesting the French government's decision to test nuclear weapons near New Zealand.

So two French spies set explosives that sank Greenpeace's ship, *Rainbow Warrior*, killing a photographer. How cheap was that? The group is called Green*peace*!

As if that wasn't bad enough, the French government denied even being involved with the sabotage. Yeesh! If only

Greenpeace had known something about self-defense. Hey, maybe its members should read this!

ASSASSINATION & SELF-DEFENSE

Like me, you're probably a nonviolent person. In my case, I know I could never stab someone—I can't even jab those sharp straws into a juice box! Even so, it's only a matter of time until someone (maybe a family member!) tries to hire you to "remove" one of his or her enemies. When this happens, remember to stay cool.

> Tough Kid (whispering): I hear you know where the bodies are buried.
>
> You (blowing a bubble with your bubblegum): And I know how to add more!

You may be tempted to accept one of these jobs, but there are a number of very good reasons to say no. First, the word "ass" is in "assassination" TWICE. This may be a sign that you should *think* twice about taking the job.

More importantly, killing people is not only illegal but also dangerous. You see, people who engage in treacherous violence often become VICTIMS of treacherous violence!

For example, two killers were once hired by Russians to assassinate a German diplomat. The assassins were each given a camera case. One camera case was red and one was blue. The assassins were told to press a button on the red case, which would activate a bomb inside of it.

After the explosion, they were to push a button on the blue case, which would lay down a smokescreen and allow them to escape.

But the assassins were suspicious. Outside of bad movies, since when is a smokescreen THAT important for a getaway? Plus, secondhand smokescreen smoke is bad for your lungs! So just to experiment, the agents pressed the button on the blue camera case. Bad move! It turned out that this case ALSO contained a bomb, and both men were blown up! (Boy, you just can't trust anyone.)

The word "assassin" comes from a group of Muslims who lived in Iran a thousand years ago. Led by Hassan i-Sabbah, these Muslims might send trained killers to stab any leader who took hostile action against them.

Today, many believe that the killers sent out on these death missions became known as "followers of Hassan," or *Assassins*. These Assassins sometimes spent years stalking their victims before finally choosing the moment of truth. So the killer needed to be able to infiltrate an enemy community with a good cover story. And when the Assassin chose his moment, he would try to stab his victim in the most public place possible. The more crowds and the more guards, the better! This would terrify people and give the Assassins a psychological edge on their enemies.

Of course, after stabbing their targets, Assassins were usually killed by bodyguards. And because of that, some historians point to the Assassins as the world's first terrorists. But that's not quite fair. The Assassins targeted leaders who had *already* attacked their group. The idea of killing innocent unarmed people (like modern terrorists do) would have been revolting to them.

Hey, maybe the Assassins SAVED lives! By killing hostile leaders, the Assassins prevented wars that would have killed far more people than ONE. And it's not like the Assassins stabbed everybody who bothered them. For instance, Hassan i-Sabbah was once concerned about a sultan who was ordering military expeditions against the Assassins.

So one morning, the sultan woke up in his bedchamber and found a dagger plunged into the floor next to his bed!

Later that day, the sultan got a message from the Assassins: *"Did I not wish the Sultan well, that dagger which was stuck into the hard ground would have been planted in his soft chest."*

Hassan didn't have any trouble from the sultan after that!

CLOAKS AND DAGGERS

The traditional symbols for spies are the cloak and the dagger. The cloak is handy for hiding things like the spy himself, as well as the dagger he is holding. (The dagger is handy for assassinations and can also be used to spread butter on toast.)

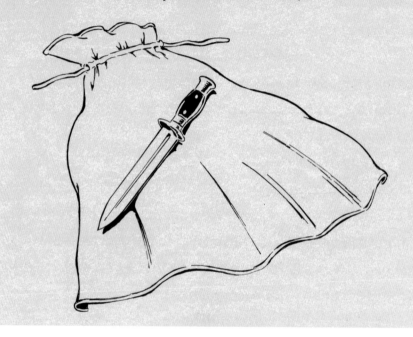

The Assassins left us their legacy today. Not just the word "assassin," but also the knowledge that even the most fantastic bodyguards can't stop a killer from getting to a leader. Because of that, there is an unspoken rule in the world today that no leader of a nation (especially a democracy) should order the assassination of ANOTHER leader. Because once someone does that, then ANYONE could be fair game and no one would be safe!

Of course, this rule doesn't apply to people who *aren't* national leaders, so assassinations continue. And one national leader was the exception to this rule—Fidel Castro, the president of Cuba.

FIDEL CASTRO: THE CIA REALLY HATED THAT GUY!

It's possible that no leader has inspired more odd assassination attempts than Castro. For example, since the Cuban leader loved to smoke cigars, CIA agents got the not-very-creative idea to use cigars to kill him! The agents came up with two plans:

1. In 1961, a Cuban double agent was given a cigar that had been poisoned with something called botulin. The spy was to give Castro the cigar, and after the Cuban leader smoked it, the botulin would kill him! But the double agent botched the botulin and it never happened.

2. A powerful exploding cigar was made to give Castro. How powerful? According to an agent, it would "blow his head off"! But this idea didn't work out.

Since the cigar ideas weren't working, CIA agents tried other ideas to kill Castro. (Boy, they really hated that guy!) These other killer attempts included a poisoned scuba-diving suit, an exploding seashell, and enlisting Mafia members to see if THEY could arrange for Castro's death.

These plans all failed. And in 1963, the all-time most insane concept was invented: a poison pen! Here's how it worked: Castro would pick it up and push down on the pen's button to get the ballpoint end to come up. When he did this, a small needle would stick out of the button, poisoning him! Then the Cuban dictator would finally die, die, DIE!

So did it work? Ha! Almost fifty years after the poison pen idea, Castro is still very much alive (as of this writing).

DEADLY WEAPONS

Despite my expertise at self-defense, I'm nursing a spy injury right now. I was gathering intelligence at a croquet tournament, and one of the balls caught me RIGHT on the ankle. Dang, those things are hard! It's like they're made of wood or something. In fact, it's clear to me that a croquet ball (or the mallet used to hit it) could be used as a death-dealing weapon of deadliness!

But what is the MOST deadly weapon that people use on a daily basis? The CAR. That's right. Each day, millions of people get behind the steering wheel and fly down the street inside of several tons of hard steel. Get in their way and you'll be crushed!

This is not to suggest that you learn how to drive so you can destroy enemy agents. But be aware that THEY might be out there gunning the engine for you! And these automotive assassins don't need to be in a minivan to do you in. For instance, here are three nonmotorized vehicles your assassin could choose instead:

BICYCLE

Danger: It's faster than you.

Good Defense: Run behind a tree.

Bad Defense: Run down the middle of the street.

Fun Fact: If the assassin runs you down, he will probably wipe out.

SKATEBOARD

Danger: Skateboarders have "no fear." (Their T-shirts even say so!)

Good Defense: Run by a skate ramp. (Skateboarders are easily distracted.)

Bad Defense: Stand at the bottom of the skate ramp.

Fun Fact: Even if you get hit, you're safe from the ankles up!

TRICYCLE

Danger: Those three wheels can leave nasty rubber marks as they go over you.

Good Defense: Avoid spots where trikers hang out, like playgrounds and triker bars.

Bad Defense: Getting on a tricycle to escape. (You're too big!)

Fun Fact: Alexander the Great never used tricycles when he conquered the world.

As you can see, by redefining what a weapon is, your enemies will try to take advantage of you. So to defend yourself when a chunky desperado confronts you with murder in his eyes and orange wax in his ears, know these three simple rules:

1. WEAPONS ARE *EVERYWHERE.* A weapon

doesn't have to be a knife or a tricycle. A banana is a weapon. True, it doesn't stab very well, and bananas rarely explode. But what if someone was chasing you and slipped on a banana peel that you had put there? I have heard of things like this happening. (Of course, I also watch a lot of cartoons.)

However, your opponents may use something more sophisticated than a banana. For instance, DARPA (see p. 36) is working on scopes for rifles that will enable snipers to shoot targets from almost two miles away—in heavy winds. And the snipers may be using bullets that can change course in midair. (Seriously.) If your enemies have one of these, you'd better have a pretty high-tech banana to protect yourself. (Or maybe a mango!)

2. LEARN BARTITSU. You're going to think I'm making this up. I'm not. In the early 1900s, a man named Edward William Barton-Wright invented a form of martial arts self-defense called Bartitsu. One of his techniques was based on the idea that weapons are EVERYWHERE. So bicyclists were encouraged to use their bikes if they were attacked!

Bartitsu experts came up with moves like riding over an attacker with the bicycle or sticking the bike pump into his armpit. And if the rider was on a folding bicycle, he could dismount and then simply fold up the attacker inside of his bike!

Of course, there are MANY other martial arts you could learn instead. So why am I recommending Bartitsu? Because it has the coolest name of all time, of course!

BARTALI DIDN'T NEED BARTITSU

Gino Bartali was a great Italian bicyclist. How great? When World War II started, Bartali had already won the Tour de France. But what role could a great biker play during wartime?

Bartali became a bicycle courier! He worked for the Italian Resistance and spent years pedaling secret messages between resistance groups while wearing his "Bartali" racing jersey. Even though Bartali was once arrested and interrogated, he wouldn't stop riding for freedom. And that's how Bartali became a war hero—and stayed in shape at the same time.

After the war, Bartali won the Tour de France again. He rarely spoke of his work during the war. But three years after he died in 2000, documents revealed that in addition to his other work, Bartali had delivered documents that helped save the lives of 800 Jews.

3. REACT, DON'T DRAW! In the unlikely event that you find yourself having to "draw" a weapon against an enemy agent, let HIM make the first move. Studies suggest that you will draw 10 percent faster if you're reacting than if you draw your own gun first. And that 10 percent should make up for your opponent's advantage.

Unless it doesn't!

4. USE *SURPRISE* TO YOUR ADVANTAGE.
For instance, what if a ninja sprang out of your closet

right now? Admittedly, if you're not reading this book in your bedroom, it wouldn't make much of an impression on you.

And if you WERE home, it would be suicidal to engage in actual hand-to-hand combat with the ninja. (Besides, it's foolish to fight with only *one* hand; next time, try hands-to-hands combat!)

Running away is also a poor choice. It is not very dignified behavior for an intelligence agent, plus you might get a ninja star thrown at your butt.

So as the ninja advances, you look quickly around you for weapons. You see a laptop, some computer cords, a number of pens and pencils, a small wastepaper basket, and an electric fan. These give you choices!

Turn the fan on high, rip off its protective cover, and chop that ninja up with its soft, rubber blades. Then dispose of the ninja pieces in the wastebasket.

Or you could hit "save" on your document and shut down your laptop properly. After that's done, detach the computer's power cable and use it as a strangling device called a *garrote* (guh-ROTE).

GARROTE DEFENSE!

Assassins like to use a garrote because it's a silent killer. The idea is that the agent approaches a guard from behind and loops a wire around the victim's neck. The agent then pulls tight until the victim stops guarding and *starts* dying!

Ah, but what if you see a garrote wire suddenly looping in front of *your* face and digging into your neck? Pay attention! If the garrote is made with a guitar string, it's a good bet that your wannabe assassin plays guitar. Lunge for a drum set and try to tap out a beat, however feeble. Your assassin will then release you! Why? Because no guitarist—not even a killer guitarist—can resist the temptation to "jam" with another musician.

On the other hand, if you're being strangled with a piano wire, you're doomed—because nobody loves playing solo more than a pianist. (Those selfish, selfish pianists!)

To avoid the difficulty of telling the difference between garrote wires, remember that if someone walks up behind you, there is a good chance they will cast a shadow. This will give you a chance to disarm the attacker *before* the attack. (Using this method, I just disarmed a waiter of a diet soda while waiting for my lunch.)

If it seems like I'm making this sound too easy, I'm not! It turns out that lots of ninjas have been sort of dorky. For example, a whole group of ninjas once tried to kill General Oda Nobunaga by shooting a cannon at him. The general was RIGHT in front of the cannon. They couldn't miss!

The ninjas missed.

This was because the ninja's usual job was *spying* and sneaking around in disguise, not killing people. And the disguises the ninjas wore were NOT black pajamas. That would be sort of a giveaway! Instead, ninjas wore farmer outfits or the uniforms of the enemy army. (One of the only successful ninja assassinations occurred when the ninja dressed as a young girl!)

The legend of the black pajamas began in the 1600s. Real ninjas were disappearing as the need for spies in Japan diminished. At the same time, stories about ninjas became popular. The Japanese had a popular live theater called Kabuki. In it, puppets acted out dramas while puppet-masters dressed in black outfits stood behind them. Since there was already a Japanese tradition of pretending that people in black were invisible, black became the color of choice in the new plays about fictional ninja assassins.

So what I'm saying is that the only ninjas to wear black pajamas have been actors!

FAKE NINJA
PAJAMAS

REAL NINJA
PAJAMAS

But if you're looking for a ninja making a real fashion statement, you should learn about the *kunoichi*. These were female ninja agents, and in addition to the usual ninja skills, they were also trained to be charming servants or entertainers. In these roles, the *kunoichi* could get into an enemy camp and then gather intelligence, poison the soup, and throw *shuriken* ("sword hidden in the hand") at anybody who annoyed them!

Plus, imagine this situation. A Japanese warlord comes upon a young woman holding a fan up to her face and weeping on the side of the road. Since men are usually more suspicious of MEN, the warlord pauses to see what's wrong.

"What's wrong?" he asks while leaning off his horse.

With a lightning-like flip, the woman flips the fan, cuts off the warlord's head, and disappears in the confusion that follows. She was a *kunoichi* with a razor-sharp fan! And her plan was totally simple, which shows what a pro she was. Because as you know, the cleverer an assassin tries to be, the more likely something will go wrong.

For example, let's say you come up with a spray gun that shoots a poisonous cyanide gas. Brilliant! There won't be any shell casings for the police to use as clues. (That's why notorious Russian agent Bogdan Stashinsky used this method.) However, this could lead to a problem:

Assassin (muttering): I'll aim the poison spray gun at my victim, and *voilà*!

Unsuspecting Victim: Hmm, the wind has shifted directions!

Assassin: Can't . . . breathe—*Urk!*

Clearly, assassins are sometimes just too clever for their own good. For example, in 1960, the CIA prepared a tube of poison toothpaste. It was to be slipped into the bathroom of the prime minister of the Congo. The CIA chief in the Congo vetoed the plan, but still—death by *toothpaste*? What next, razor-sharp dental floss?

"IT'S FOR YOU."

Some villains are so mean, their assassination seems only fair. This may be true in the case of Yahya Ayyash. As the main bomb-builder for a Mideast terrorist group, Ayyash was responsible for the deaths of over a hundred innocent Israeli civilians. (His skill with explosives earned him the nickname "The Engineer.")

To rid themselves of The Engineer, Israeli agents came up with a plan. In 1996, they made a bugged cell phone that was also loaded with explosives. The agents then tricked a friend of Ayyash's into giving him the phone. And since the phone's bug revealed when the terrorist was speaking into it, the Israeli agents knew when to activate. And they did.

THE WHITE DEATH

In 2010, the CIA fired a drone missile the size of a violin at a terrorist in Pakistan. The missile was directed by agents *outside of* the country as it successfully hit its target. This changed the world of assassination forever. After all, now an assassin could be located in a different continent from his quarry!

I wonder what Simo Häyhä would make of that. He was a farmer living in Finland when Russia invaded his country in 1939. To defend his homeland, Häyhä became a sniper. Dressed in white to blend in with the Finnish winter, Häyhä went off into the woods and started picking off enemy soldiers. And despite the fact that he was only about five feet tall, Häyhä soon became the greatest sniper of all time! Not only was he an amazing shot, but he had a number of tricks for staying hidden from the enemy. For instance, Häyhä held snow in his mouth while in the field, so that when he was breathing, the steam of his breath would not give away his location.

And in just over three months, Häyhä shot and killed between 700 and 800 Russian soldiers. The Russians were terrified! They nicknamed Häyhä "The White Death" and sent special squads out to kill him. Those IDIOTS. You can't kill the White Death! So, the anti-Häyhä squads never returned. Can you guess why?[1]

---

1. Häyhä shot them.

Finally, Häyhä caught a Russian bullet in the head. The timing of this was odd because he was found the same day that peace was declared between Finland and Russia. Anyway, Häyhä shouldn't have survived his wound. After all, when he was found, he was missing the entire left side of his face. But

that's nothing to the White Death! Häyhä was not only nursed back to health but went on to live until he was 97 years old.

THE ASSASSIN WITH A HEART

Let's end with a feel-good story. Nikolai Khokhlov was a trained Russian assassin who was assigned to kill a man named Georgi Okolovich, an anti-Communist living in Germany. Khokhlov was armed for the job with an unusual gun: it was electrically operated, made no more noise than the snap of your fingers, fit inside a cigarette case, and fired poison-tipped bullets that might lead a coroner to think the victim had died of heart failure.

In 1954, the Russian assassin knocked on Okolovich's apartment door. There, Khokhlov confessed that he had been sent to murder him . . . but his wife had talked him out of it! I'd imagine that this was a strange conversation for Okolovich.

Khokhlov: I was sent here to assassinate you, but my wife thinks it's a bad idea.

Okolovich: Can you come back later? Wait—don't come back later!

Khokhlov: Don't worry. I have a conscience, and I'm not going to do it.

Okolovich: Well, THAT'S nice to hear. Would you like a crumpet?

Okolovich ended up inviting Khokhlov inside, and the two men tried to figure out what to do about the strange situation in which they found themselves. As a result of their meeting, Nikolai Khokhlov defected to the West. He gave press conferences and wrote a book (*In the Name of Conscience*) about his training as an assassin.

But three years later, Khokhlov himself fell mysteriously ill. It turned out that the former assassin was himself the victim of an assassination attempt! The Russian had been poisoned by a radioactive substance. (Specifically, someone had put a nuclear isotope of thallium into his cup of coffee.)

But after getting massive blood transfusions, Khokhlov survived. He moved to California and taught at a university. The Assassin with a Heart ended up living well into the 21st century.

SECRET MESSAGES
& Code-Breaking

Spying is a game of punch and counterpunch. So if I write a secret message, you would counterpunch by trying to *read* it. And if I use a secret code, you'd respond by trying to *decode* my code. And if I lightly punched your arm because this annoys me, you'd counterpunch and give me a *charley horse*.

And that isn't fair, because a charley horse hurts WAY worse than a little punch in the arm!

But as we've learned, the life of a spy can be tough. After all, we can't rely on ANYONE to be honest. Even ourselves! Imagine you're sitting at home and a postcard pops through the mail slot. Picking it up (*"Ooh, Hawaii!"*), you see that the postcard is addressed to your sister.

So you read it!

You would, wouldn't you? After all, it would be VERY tempting. Reading someone else's messages is so irresistible that the French government created something called the *Post aux Lettres* in 1590. The mission of this department wasn't to *deliver* the mail. It was to *read* everyone's mail. (What a great job!)

But where the French excel, American intelligence has sometimes lagged. Secretary of State Henry L. Stimson even shut down the United States code-breaking operation in 1929. Stimson's explanation for why he did this was that "Gentlemen do not read each other's mail."

Clearly, Mr. Stimson was NOT French.

If you want to learn secrets, reading someone's snail mail, email, or texts will do it. That's why 2,300 years ago, Alexander the Great encouraged his soldiers to write home a LOT. Alexander then had his intelligence agents read the letters to check on troop morale.

The spies reading this mail knew they needed to worry about their own messages home. And this led to the invention of codes. A code gives a secret meaning to the symbols in a message. And the use of codes is called *cryptography*.[1]

★ Creepies? In the spy world, code experts are known as cryptologists, or "crippies."

PSST! WANT TO MAKE A CODE?

The key to *this* code is to start in the top left corner. Counting that letter "S" as one, count off till you hit 13. That letter is the first one of your message. Now count another 13, and that letter is the next one, and so on.

This message is

Convoy
leaves
thursday.

```
S h e e o o
Y         a
N         r
Y         t
A         v
S u d c v l
```

Now figure out this one!

```
Y v a u h o
D         o
U         r
N         e
T         s
R e g d g n
```

---

1. *Codes* are different from *ciphers,* which substitute a different letter or number for each letter or number you see.

˙pooƃʎɹǝʌǝsʇnuɥƃnoᗡ sᴉ ǝƃɐssǝɯ ǝɥꓕ

In the 5th Century BCE, the Greek tyrant Histiaeus devised a clever new way to send hidden messages. He shaved the head of one of his servants, tattooed a message on his head, and waited for the man's hair to grow back. Then the messenger was sent on his way.

When the courier arrived at his destination, his head was shaved again and the message was read, giving information about upcoming Persian attacks. (It was "Not Very" Instant Messaging!)

Anyway, Histiaeus may have been the first person to use *steganography*, the practice of hiding one message within something else entirely. In other words, no one knows the message is there except for the person the message is FOR. In this way, *steganography* is better than *cryptography*, because an encrypted message can look suspicious. *"Look at all those weird letters and symbols . . . we'd better figure them out!"*

Here's how innocent steganography can be: An agent once secretly knitted a message into a wool sweater by using Morse code in its patterns. Now, who's so paranoid that they'd be suspicious of a sweater? No one!

The word "steganography" was coined by a German monk back in the 1400s. The monk wrote a book series called *Steganographia*. But although his books LOOKED like they were about magic, there was a whole other book about secret codes hidden within them. That means that *Steganographia* was itself an example of steganography!

In 1968, a U.S. ship called the *Pueblo* was captured by North Korea. Its crew members were held for nearly a year. To prove they were still alive and healthy, the North Koreans took photos of the Americans. And since the North Koreans didn't know any North American "sign" language, the U.S. crew members added a little bit of steganography to their poses. (Let's just say the sailors were gesturing with their middle fingers!)

More recently, a group of ten Russian spies were arrested in the United States in 2010. These spies had lived in the States for over ten years, and nobody aside from FBI agents suspected them of wrongdoing. One way the spies communicated was by embedding secret code into ordinary photos. These images were then posted on public websites like Facebook, where other spies could download and decipher them.

This Russian spy story spawned the greatest quote in the history of the world. One of the suspects went by the name Cynthia Murphy, and she was known as a master gardener. So after the FBI arrested the spies, one of Mrs. Murphy's neighbors said, "They *couldn't* have been spies. [I mean] look what she did with the hydrangeas."[2]

I think that if there's a place for hydrangeas and other flowers in spying, then there must also be a place for fashion accessories. You know, like handbags, earrings, and paperclips.

Let me explain!

The paperclip was invented by a man from Norway named Johann Valer. Although it might be hard for you to understand, Valer's paperclip then became a symbol of national pride for Norwegians, sort of like an American flag button or a Union Jack T-shirt.

During World War II, the Nazis took over Norway. That meant the Norwegians who were still secretly fighting the Nazis needed an easy way to display their loyalty. But what a

---

2. One of these Russian spies once found it necessary to write down a false address. The trained professional then wrote "99 Fake Street."

challenge! Secret handshakes were out, and T-shirts saying "The Nazis conquered my country and all I got was this lousy T-shirt" seemed a little too obvious.

But some Norwegian genius—perhaps an office supplies manager—came up with the idea of just putting a paperclip on his collar. And THAT became the secret sign that the freedom fighters used!

There are lots of ways to put your message into code. Roman emperor Julius Caesar came up with one of the first and simplest systems. All you do is write the alphabet out. Then below it, write the alphabet out again, but start it in a different spot. In other words, for the second alphabet, you might put A below L. When writing your code, you simply substitute the letters for each other. Using this version of the **Caesar cipher,** M would be substituted for a B, and W would be used instead of an L.

A B C D E F G H I J K L M N O P Q R S T U V W X Y Z

P Q R S T U V W X Y Z A B C D E F G H I J K L M N O

Sure, it's easy to break the Caesar cipher nowadays. But in ancient times, this code worked especially well because most people couldn't read. (Those ninnies!) Speaking of reading, my favorite cipher method is the **Book Code.** First, you need a book—and, coincidentally, you're reading one right now.

NO, SERIOUSLY. DO YOU WANT TO MAKE A CODE OR NOT?

For this easy code, all you have to do is find 26 words from a poem or song you like. Then assign each word from the lyrics a letter! To get started, I chose a 26 word poem by W. B. Yeats: "And though I would have hushed the crowd/There was no mother's son but said/'What is the figure in the shroud/upon a gaudy bed?'"

This poem only has *one* repeated word: "the." Since that word is repeated *three* times, that means I need to *add* two new words to the poem. (I've added "big" and "soft" below.) That way, each letter of the alphabet has its own corresponding letter.

My poem's code would look like this:

And	although	I	would	have	hushed	the	crowd
A	B	C	D	E	F	G	H

There	was	no	mother's	son	but	said,
I	J	K	L	M	N	O

"What	is	the	figure	in	the	shroud
P	Q	R	S		T	

upon	a	big,	soft,	gaudy	bed?"
U	V	W	X	Y	Z

Now you have to share this code with a friend. Once you both have it, you can text or write short notes to each other. These notes will look like gibberish to anyone without the code! For example, decode this (or just look at the footnote): *"Hushed-there-the but-have-big-shroud-said-but-in and-figure-have the-said-said-would."*[3]

---

3. Translation: "Fig newtons are good."

Then, you make sure the person you're going to send the code to has the SAME book in his or her possession. (So buy another copy of this book!)

Open to any page and note the page number. Now look at the words on it. (I know this sounds stupid, but trust me.) The words on the page are what you're going to use to create your message. Of course, for your message to be *decoded*, you will need to tell your agent where to look. So the message might read:

> 264 [*this is the page number*]
>
> 7/6, 9/5, 16/1, 1/4, 5/2, 4/6, 10/8 [*these are the line numbers and the order of the words within the lines*]

Of course, **invisible ink** is a classic way to hide messages. When using paper for these, almost any acid, like lemon juice or vinegar, will work. (Urine has also been used for centuries, but I don't recommend it!) The acids will weaken the fibers in the paper. And when the paper is held up to a candle or strong light, the heat will highlight these weakened portions, revealing the message. But be careful! Many secret messages have disappeared into ash because someone held the paper too close to the candle. So use a blow dryer to get your invisible writing to appear instead.

You don't have to have a handwritten document to use invisible ink! Try this: open a document or email on a computer. Now write a "secret message." When you're done, highlight your whole message and go to the word-processing tool that selects font color. Choose the white color, and watch your whole message disappear! Then send the message to your contact.

When she gets the message, your contact just needs to "Select all" and change the font color to black! What follows is an example of what I mean. If you can decipher the following invisible ink message using these instructions, you're eligible to win $100,000. Here it is, and good luck:

If you're worried that sending a blank document to someone is too suspicious, just write a seemingly double-spaced message. Actually, it will be SINGLE-spaced, and you'll alternate lines. One line will be written in black, one line will be written in white, and so forth.

This isn't unlike the way that real invisible ink works. If a person were suspected of spying and she had several sheets of "blank" paper with her, it would look suspicious. That's why it's common for pages with invisible ink to have pictures or other text in VISIBLE ink on them! For example, Josephine Baker was a famous singer who routinely carried sheet music with her to performances during World War

II. This provided a nice way to transport secret notes throughout Nazi-controlled Europe.

You see, along with the music, Baker's sheets had invisible ink messages written on them!

Hey, that reminds me of a joke.
> Q. Do you know how to read invisible ink?
> A. Wear invisible glasses.

If you think that, like that joke, invisible ink is too lame for any real spy to use, think again! In the United States, top secret documents eventually get "declassified." That means anyone can read them. But in 1999, the CIA stated that the invisible ink using lemon juice (which agents have been using for centuries) was to remain outside of the declassification process. Why? Because this kind of invisible ink was still being used!

During World War II, German intelligence agents put secret messages into code using something called the Enigma machine. Because it was so sophisticated, and since its settings were changed daily, it was assumed that nobody would ever figure it out. But the British had a genius mathematician named Alan Turing, who designed the world's first computer. Named the Bombe, it was able to decipher the German code. Yes! Intercepting and understanding German messages meant that tens of thousands of lives were saved.

What makes this even better is that Turing was a kooky genius. He was known for chaining his tea mug to radiators so his coworkers wouldn't steal it. Turing sometimes ran the 40 miles between London and his workplace for meetings. And when he rode his bike, Turing wore a gas mask to avoid getting hay fever.

MIDDLE EARTH HUMOR

A year after *The Hobbit* was published, author J. R. R. Tolkien trained as a code-breaker where Alan Turing worked. But for an unknown reason, Tolkien didn't stick with the program. This led one historian to joke, "Perhaps it was because we declared war on Germany and not Mordor."

If you ever want to recruit a code-breaker, make sure she's good at chess AND music AND math. It turns out that the best code-breakers have been talented at all three. Or, just hire a REALLY good computer programmer. Because in today's world of codes, supercomputers do the majority of enciphering and deciphering messages.

For example, the computers used at the National Security Agency (NSA) in the United States are believed to have more power than anywhere on the planet. (The NSA has acres and acres and acres of computers.) And guess what the NSA's in charge of?[4]

4. Codes and ciphers!

SPYMASTERS

A spymaster is the person in charge of an entire group of agents. And while it's nice to have the title "Spymaster" on your business card, it's an incredibly difficult job.

It's the topsy-turvy logic that makes spying so hard! For example, imagine that you are a spymaster. An enemy agent approaches you and says she wants to work for you. How could you know that she wasn't a deliberate plant who is going to give you false information? You wouldn't! So you'd almost HAVE to hire her. And then you'd have to watch that double agent carefully!

★ *The Deadliest Game:* British agents nicknamed their spymasters "gamekeepers."

Let's look at some famous spymasters, starting with . . .

THE SPY-DERMASTER

What spymaster wove the most tangled web? That might have been Reinhard Gehlen (1902–1979). He was a head of Nazi intelligence during World War II. But Gehlen knew that Germany might lose the war, so he buried steel drums full of intelligence information on Russia just in case.

After Germany DID lose, Gehlen surrendered to the Allied forces. Gehlen was brought back to West Germany, where his steel drums were dug up. Impressed with his intelligence, the Americans put Gehlen in charge of a new spy network. (Not everyone approved; one American general called it "that spooky Nazi outfit.") And after that, Gehlen also helped countries like Egypt and Israel with their intelligence.

So how many countries did Gehlen do spy work for? At LEAST five . . . and probably more!

WHO KNEW?

Many high-ranking Nazis who were caught after World War II were *not* imprisoned or executed. Instead, countries like the United States and Great Britain used them as scientists and spies.

MOSES—THE ORIGINAL SPYMASTER

Moses was one of the earliest spymasters we know of. And his first operation was a disaster!

Many people believe that Moses led the Jews out of Egypt over 3,000 years ago. The idea was for the Jews to head for the Holy Land. So Moses sent 12 spies ahead of the main group to gather intelligence on anyone who might be living there.

But some of these spies were captured. And the ones who did return gave different reports of what they had seen. This might not have been so bad, but Moses had the spies give their reports *publicly* in front of all the Jews!

Only two of these spies recommended that the Jews go forth and try to take over the Holy Land. And some of the spies said the Holy Land was now occupied by *giants.* Everyone panicked! This led to no decision and contributed to 40 years of dithering around in the wilderness.

So we see that Moses faced two classic problems that a spymaster faces:

1. What do you do when your spies don't agree with each other?
2. How do you keep a secret a *secret*?

Joshua took over after Moses, and he had better success. Using experienced spies that reported only to him, Joshua conquered the city of Jericho. And thousands of years later, the CIA did a report comparing these two Jewish spymasters. (Really!) The CIA report concluded:

Moses used amateur spies that reported in public.
Result: The people lost confidence and went on to suffer a long period of severe punishment.
Joshua used professional spies that reported in private.
Result: The secret agents helped Joshua achieve his national goals.

THE SPYMASTER THAT WAS AFRAID OF HIS EMPLOYEES

In a spy's treacherous world, it takes some pretty dastardly deeds for a spy group to stand out. But one Russian agency does: the dreaded *Oprichniki*! This secret police force was formed by Czar Ivan the Terrible in 1565. Their job was to find Russians who were unhappy with Czar Ivan the Terrible and then crush them! (I don't know about you, but I wouldn't be anxious to mess with anyone nicknamed "the Terrible" in the first place.)

The members of the Oprichniki rode black horses, dressed in black, and had the emblem of a dog's head and a broom on their black saddles. Their mission was to use spies to "sniff out" those who dared question the czar's authority and then "sweep them" up and throw them away. How does one sweep up humans? By stealing their land and then imprisoning or executing them.

Also known as the "Czar's dogs," the Oprichniki were so good at their dreadful job that Ivan the Terrible himself grew frightened of them. So he disbanded the secret police and scattered the Oprichniki agents. Then just to make sure nobody remembered them, Ivan the Terrible made a terrible new law: anyone who even *said* the word "Oprichniki" was executed!

MY FAVORITE SPYMASTER OF ALL TIME!

Juan Pujol García (1912–1988) watched in dismay as Nazi Germany took over Europe in the 1930s. So in 1940, García offered to work as a spy for the British.

But the Brits rejected him. Uncool!

García then offered to work as a spy for the *Germans*. And they hired him!

Once he got this job, García applied for a *second* time to the British. This time, the Brits were only too happy to take on a double agent that was this creative! And García was just getting started. He developed a spy network of 27 agents that collected information for the Nazis. There was just one catch: the spies were all imaginary! (These kinds of fake agents are sometimes called "notional spies.")

To make his fake spies realistic, García had to invent a believable life story for each one. And once that work was done, García began creating a symphony of false intelligence. The tricks he played on the Germans saved thousands of lives during the war.

Speaking of lives, García once "killed off" one of his imaginary agents and ran a death notice in a British newspaper. In that way, he managed to convince the Germans to pay a pension to the man's imaginary widow.

THE AGENTS OF JUAN PUJOL GARCÍA

Best of all, García was one of the only people ever to be given medals by both the Germans AND the British during World War II. Now if that isn't a good spymaster, I don't know what is!

Keeping Secrets
SECRET!

Nearly a million people in the United States alone have top secret clearance. And you should be one of them! When you apply for a job as a spy, agents will run a background check on you. That means they'll be interviewing people who know you. And one of the most important questions your friends and family will be asked is, "Can [your name] keep a *secret*?"

The sad thing is, if you don't ALREADY know how to keep a secret, you'll probably never be able to. You can either do it or you can't! Experts believe that starting about age six, kids start to understand the idea of keeping a secret. Children who "get it" can then become trustworthy. This is why you can never expect a little kid to keep a secret! (This is also why I refuse to hire any spy under the age of six.)

But sometimes, even older spies just don't get it. One wannabe agent confidently told me, "I know what a secret is."

"Okay," I said, "what IS a secret?"

Wrong.

I fired that kid before he even had the job![1] At least he knew that once you HAVE a secret, it's tempting to tell somebody. But if you ever want to get a top-security clearance, you must RESIST that temptation.

I encourage you to think about the power you have when you keep a secret. It's a power you only get by never repeating rumors or gossip. Seriously! It shows that you're trustworthy, and that's how you get to the point where people will trust you with their secrets.

Oh, and avoid those people who always try to drag gossip out of you. Who needs the aggravation? If somebody really pushes it, go with the standard spy non-answer: *"I can neither confirm nor deny it."* This is good! It's not a lie and no information is given. Practice using this line!

---

1. I felt bad, though, so I gave him a different job as my life coach.

SECRETS REVEALED!

One of the strangest things in the history of secrets happened in Germany. After World War II, the country was divided into *West* Germany (a free democracy) and *East* Germany (a communist country controlled by Russia). The East German government kept a constant eye on its citizens. Its leaders were worried that the East Germans would either flee to the West or become spies.

But in 1990, the two Germanys were reunited! That meant there was no need for the old East German spy agency called the Stasi. And then a politician named Vera Wollenberger passed a law that opened Stasi's top secret files to the public.

Wow! Parents learned that their children had spied on them—and vice-versa! A famous human rights worker was discovered to be a spy. There was even a man who learned that his depression came from the drugs his own *doctor* prescribed him. (The Stasi had ordered the doctor to do this.)

As for Vera Wollenberger, she was surprised to discover that her own HUSBAND was a Stasi informant! Downer. (How do you say "divorce" in German?)

ROSKO! EVEN YOU?

Why were there so many spies and informers? Some people were pressured into it. And an expert said that most "people informed for personal gain, out of loyalty, or simply because they wanted to feel like they had some power."

Germany is still recovering from this avalanche of secrets, which is maybe a good lesson. We should be careful about wanting to know secrets—because we might not like what we discover! (Even so, I still think I'd like to see the FBI files on my family. You see, I have a sneaking suspicion about my brother . . .)

BUT WHO GETS TO KNOW WHAT?

The next time you play miniature golf or enter the octagon for a mixed martial arts match, think of your opponent as the Government. And pretend that you're a Reporter! This will help motivate you to win, because Reporters LOVE to uncover secrets. And the Government loves to KEEP secrets.

That means they're archenemies!

But should one side always win against the other? I mean, there are some government secrets that citizens *should* know. But it's impossible to share those secrets with citizens while also keeping them from the government's *enemies*.

Although there are many arguments over this, here are some things that almost always need to STAY secret:
- Codes and ciphers
- Identity of spies
- Location and movement of troops
- Location and movement of satellites and classified weapons.

HE REALLY DISLIKED REPORTERS

Union General William Sherman hated newspaper reporters. Sherman even once tried to have a newsman shot for "spying" on his troops during the Civil War. (The writer was actually just working on a story.) And upon hearing that three reporters had been killed by artillery, Sherman said, "Good, now we shall have news from hell before breakfast."

If an important secret *is* going to be outed, the good should outweigh the bad. For instance, in the 1960s, the U.S. government had a secret plan to invade Cuba. Even though the *New York Times* learned about this plan, the newspaper chose NOT to print the story because American lives might be lost if they did.

So the *Times* sat on the secret. And the Cuban invasion was a total disaster! Not only didn't it work, but lots of people died. Furthermore, the invasion was so lame, the United States looked idiotic for a long time afterwards.

So it would have been a lot better for everyone if the *Times* HAD printed the secret story—but how could its writers have known?

Interestingly, there are times when a secret is so important, it's the SPIES who leak them to a news organization. And if a SPY thinks people should know something, I guess they probably should!

Finally, here's a secret about secrets: after a while, they lose all their power! Think about it. What was your most embarrassing secret when you were five? Perhaps you got caught picking your nose in class. Or maybe you wet your bed at a sleepover. Who cares! (Please ignore these examples if you are six.) The point is, the all-important secrets that spies die for today are often just *interesting* secrets in a few short years.

And that's why I can't think of ANY secret that should be kept secret forever. Even the fact that I love cupcakes with pink frosting. (Hey, don't laugh. You picked your nose in kindergarten!)

THE BEST
(and Worst!)
Secret Names Ever

"The Great Game." That's the name that British agents once used for spy work. And espionage *is* like a game. For example, in Monopoly when you pass "Go," you get interrogated if you can't explain exactly WHY you have an extra $200. (That's how we play at my house, anyway.)

Once you get your top secret clearance, you'll be joining a group of other intelligence agents. So what cool code name should you call yourselves? There are different approaches you could take. For instance, the CIA is sometimes called "The Company" or "The Firm." *Bor-ring.* And there's a private spy agency called "The Analysis Corporation." That's even more of a snoozer!

But I've discovered that these names are lame on purpose. The idea is that if an agency's name is generic enough, people won't notice that these places even exist. So spies are always on the look-out for the most boring ways to describe their offices and agencies.

My research shows that the most boring phrases in the English language are "country music," "math homework," and "basket expert." So the CIA should change its name to something like the CMBE: "Country Music Basket Experts."

Once it does this, the spy agency will become magically invisible!

So spies like boring names. Why else would they call themselves "assets"? They do, you know, as in "we have an asset in their government." (So if you ever hit a spymaster's agent with your foot, you've kicked his asset!) But if you want to keep things REALLY secret, give your spy group an INSULTING code name. For example, what if you called your agency "the Idiots"? Nobody would want to join—in fact, people would avoid you.

> Suspicious Person: Hey, what are you guys talking about?
>
> You: It's just a meeting of the Idiots. Do you want to be an Idiot?
>
> Suspicious Person (*backing away*): No thanks! I'll see you Idiots later.

A good example of this is the Bigot List. In World War II, people in the Allied Command who had access to high-level secrets were on the Bigot List. And naturally, no one else wanted to be added to the Bigot List, so they kept their distance.

On the other hand, you might want MORE members in your secret group. If so, give it the coolest name possible! That's what the founders of the Black Dragon Society did. This Japanese group was formed in 1901. And its leader was named the Darkside Emperor. Ooh, let me sign up! Wait, it was abolished in 1945? Rats.

And then there was the Chinese group from the late 1800s known as the Society of Harmonious Fists (a.k.a. the Boxers). Good one!

Here's one of the longest names I've seen: Extraordinary Commission for the Struggle Against Counter-Revolution,

Espionage, Speculation, and Sabotage. The Russians chose that name for their secret police agency in 1917.

They called it "Cheka" for short.

One of the most sinister group names in the first half of the 20th century was the Japanese agency known as the Thought Police. Also known as the Thought Section, it was charged with making sure that people didn't think . . . bad . . . thoughts. (You don't want to know how they went about figuring this out.)

And one of the best job titles ever came from an Allied unit during World War II. Called the London Controlling Station, the agency's job was to trick German military leaders. So the head of the LCS was called "the Controller of Deception."

Did you see that? The Controller of Deception! That title is so incredible, I just had to sit down. And after I did, I was inspired to research other interesting code names and spy names from spying history. Like these:

- Any specialist in the U.S. military is called a "puke." So intelligence agents are known as "*intel pukes.*"

- Morris Cohen, an agent who worked in China, was known as "Two-Gun." Can you guess why? Oh, I'll just tell you. It was because he always carried TWO guns.

👁 Sir William Reginald Hall (a British spymaster) was known as "Blinker" because of a tic that caused him to constantly wink.

👁 A New York politician named Samuel Dickstein offered to sell secrets to the Russians. But after getting paid, Dickstein never delivered. His Russian code name: "Crook."

👁 The dreaded Tai Li of Chinese military intelligence was called "The Butcher."

👁 During the Cold War, spymaster Markus Wolf (1923–2006) managed 4,000 agents for the East German agency known as Stasi. Wolf was so good, he was considered the greatest spymaster in the world. For example, he was able to place an agent as a top aide to West Germany's chancellor. (This is like someone planting an agent as vice president of the United States.) For over twenty years, nobody in the West was even sure what he looked like, so Wolf was known as "The Man Without a Face."

👁 During World War II, the Japanese had a spy in New York nicknamed "Doll Woman." She was Velvalee Dickinson, the owner of a doll shop. (This was a great cover, BTW.)

👁 The Nazis were big fans of opera singer Margery Booth. But what the Nazis didn't know was that Booth helped

British prisoners smuggle information by hiding it in her "knickers" (that is, her underpants). In fact, Booth once performed for Adolf Hitler with secret intelligence in her underwear. Her nickname: the Knicker Spy!

◉ The Russians once had a spy in the United States code-named "Good Girl." (She wasn't.)

◉ Legendary Israeli agent Rafael Eitan was once involved in an operation where he had to travel through sewers to blow up a radar station. This earned him the nickname "Rafi the Smelly."

◉ Russian security head Nikolai Ezhov was known as "The Bloodthirsty Dwarf." (He was five feet tall.)

◉ And NBA player Jameer Nelson was nicknamed "Crib Midget" by his teammate Dwight Howard. Admittedly, Nelson was never a spy, but "Crib Midget" is too cool a name not to use every chance I get!

One of the best operation code names EVER had to do with fake Allied offensives in World War II. "Operation Hambone" started in 1944. In it, an actor was hired to play a British commander. The actor went to locations in Africa and Europe, where he pretended to be planning an invasion in southern Europe. (D-Day would actually be launched on the beaches of Normandy on the northwest coast of France.)

IT'S A NOIR, NOIR WORLD

The French word *noir* (nwahr) means "black" or "dark." It's so cool, when the dreaded French spymaster Cardinal Richelieu (1585–1642) created his dastardly intelligence cabinet, he called it the *Cabinet Noir*, the "Black Cabinet." Over time, *noir* has become an excellent word to use for all things dark and sinister!

THE BLACK CABINET

★ *bête noire* (bate nwahr): a person or thing that one particularly dislikes (for example, "Spies wearing spandex body suits are my *bête noire*").

★ *film noir*: a movie with a strong, dark mood (for instance, *High School Musical*).

★ *cartoon noir*: a cartoon with a strong, dark mood (such as *The Little Mermaid*).

The awesomeness of *noir* has inspired spies through the years. For instance, after World War I, the United States created an intelligence agency called the American Black Chamber. Scary!

You should know that intelligence agents and military people love to use INITIALS instead of names. The string of initials is called an *acronym*. These acronyms are popular because the official names for things can be really long and clumsy.

Sometimes these initials are so catchy, the original name gets forgotten. So instead of saying, "Sir, I've got the agent's Point of Origin," a spy could just say, "I've got the agent's POO!" (This is a real acronym, BTW.) Happily for us, the good people at the "Danger Zone" website have collected some acronyms for us.

BaTMAN	Biochronicity and Temporal Mechanisms Arising in Nature
RoBIN	Robustness of Biologically Inspired Networks
GODZILA	Game-theoretic Optimal Deformable Zone including Inertia with Local Approach
LOCO	Local Control of Chemistry
DISCO	Defense Industrial Security Clearance Office
DUDE	Dual-Mode Detector Ensemble
COW-PI ("cow-pie")	Compression Osmosis Water Purification Installation
NICECAP	National Intelligence Community Enterprise Cyber Assurance Program
PAST-A	Pedagogically Adaptive Scenarios for Training—Automated!
CHILI	Compact High-Resolution Infrared Long-Wave Imager

Finally, here's my favorite acronym:

AARG	Affordable Accurate Robot Guidance

Oh, last thing! During World War II, nobody in Japan could even SAY the name of the Japanese Army's spy agency ("Tokumu Bu") without being arrested. That means this HAS to have happened:

"Where do you work?"

"I'd rather not say."

"Seriously, you can trust me."

"It's not a good idea."

"Pretty please?"

"Well . . . " [*looks around nervously*], "I work for Tokumu Bu."

"You're under arrest."

SPY-CATCHING
and Lie-Detecting

Have you ever heard the old saying "It takes a thief to catch a thief"? That makes NO sense. Does it take a baker to catch a baker? No! A *butcher* could catch a baker. (But strangely, the butcher is not very good at finding the candlestick maker.)

But maybe it *does* take a spy to catch a spy, and this is why "counterintelligence" was developed. Counterintelligence agencies are in charge of hunting enemy spies and double agents.

And when counterintelligence agents spring into action, they have one thing going for them: enemy spies *stink*.

Of course, EVERYONE stinks. But the key is that we all stink in our own unique way. That's why the East German spy agency Stasi kept a "smell jar" for its suspects. This was a big jar filled with the person's personal items. The idea was that they would smell like the suspect. And if the suspect tried to flee the country, a Stasi hound dog could sniff the Smell Jar and track the person.

To get items for the smell jar, Stasi agents would break into a person's apartment when he or she wasn't home and steal them. According to Stasi agents, the best "smell item" to get was dirty laundry . . . especially dirty underwear. (That REALLY smells like the person.)

So East German counterintelligence agents stole dirty underwear. (Man, spy work is sure glamorous!)

Luckily, today's spy agencies are trying to improve on this system. For example, DARPA (see p. 36) has been trying to develop electronic noses ("e-noses") that can identify specific smells coming from terrorist armpits. (Seriously.) But sometimes you may NOT want to sniff out an enemy spy. (Warning! If you're squeamish, skip the next two paragraphs.)

In the 1980s, American workers were helping to build the new U.S. embassy in Moscow. But the Americans were convinced that when they left their hotel rooms, Russian agents were going through their belongings.

To test this, one man booby-trapped his luggage. If someone opened his suitcase, the intruder would get sprayed with shaving cream. Upon returning to the room after work, the American was pleased to see that there WAS shaving cream all over the place. Got him! But the American was then unhappy to see that a surprised and angry Russian agent had pooped on the worker's clothes.

Blech! That is so nasty, I'm going to change the subject. So here's a question: Do you think becoming a "doomed spy" would be a bad career choice?

Here's why I ask. About 2,500 years ago, a Chinese king named Ho Lu hired Sun Tzu to be his general. Good move! Sun Tzu began one of the world's first espionage agencies. Among the intelligence jobs Sun Tzu created, the *worst* one was the "doomed spy." This was a regular spy who was given totally false intelligence. The catch was that the doomed spy didn't know it was false!

The idea was that the doomed spy was sent to spy on the enemy. And once the doomed spy started his work, someone from his OWN side would expose him to the enemy.

The doomed spy was then captured and interrogated. At some point, he would probably spill all of his "secrets." This accomplished two things:

1. The enemy got *false* information but thought it was true!

2. Since the enemy had already caught a spy, it might stop searching for more of them. That meant China's

REAL spies could go to work with fewer worries of getting caught!

So now you can see why the doomed spies were really doomed.

Today, the CIA is much nicer to its spies. These agents often work under a "government cover." That means when spies are in other countries, they can pose as regular U.S. government employees. These official spies are also known as "legals" and even "gentleman spies." And this government cover gives the spies a super-power called "diplomatic immunity."

DIPLOMATIC IMMUNITY?

In 2010, a man named Mohammed al-Madadi snuck into the bathroom of an airplane to smoke. But that's against the law, so the air marshal on the flight confronted al-Madadi about it. Al-Madadi denied smoking but then made a joke about starting a fire with his shoes.

Not funny! There have been terrorists who tried to hide bombs in their shoes. So al-Madadi was arrested. But witnesses noted that al-Madadi didn't seem to care. Why was he so calm? *Diplomatic immunity.* Mohammed al-Madadi knew he probably couldn't get in any *real* trouble because he was a diplomat!

Yes, ambassadors *in any country* can commit *any* crime—from smoking on an airplane to murder—without being *charged* with the crime! Of course, no diplomat has ever gone around murdering people. If he did, he'd probably be fired from his job. And without diplomatic immunity, the diplomat might have to go to court after all.

How can this work for you? The next time you are stopped for committing sabotage on a tuna casserole, just claim "diplomatic immunity." (And if anyone asks to see your credentials, just say you left them at the embassy!)

That means if one of these official CIA spies gets caught spying (or doing any other naughty activity), he or she cannot be punished. The worst thing that can happen is the spy can be kicked out of the country, or "deported." A spy who's deported is known as a *persona non grata*: "An unwelcome person."

The number of spies that get declared *persona non grata* varies from year to year. But in 1971 alone, Great Britain expelled 105 suspected spies!

But if a CIA agent is NOT working under a government cover, everything changes. These spies have what's called a "commercial cover." (They are also sometimes called "illegals.") That means they are pretending to work for *private* companies. And if a spy gets caught while under commercial cover, he can be arrested, imprisoned, and even executed.[1]

Other cover varieties include:

Deep Cover: Agents under deep cover are put in place years before they are needed. Known as "sleeper agents," these spies are always the last ones that anyone suspects. Years ago, East Germany planted 20,000 sleeper agents in other countries. I wonder if any are still out there.

Shallow Cover: When a trained agent submerges in the 3-foot end of the swimming pool, he's surprisingly hard to spot.

Under Cover: The spy at the top of the next page is catching up on her sleep. Do not disturb.

Snap Cover: A convenient lid for Tupperware.

All these cover choices means that catching a spy is not easy. You have to be tricky! After Germany invaded France

---

1. Some U.S. spies even have *three* identities: a government cover, a commercial cover, and their true identity as CIA agents.

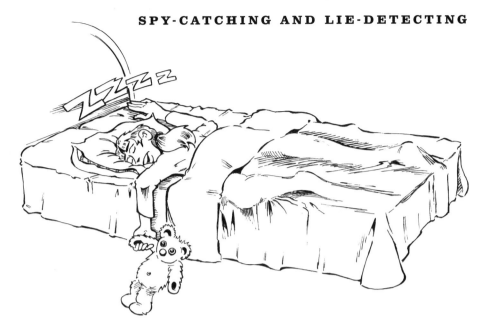

during World War II, German agents were constantly trying to catch members of the French Resistance. The French agents communicated about their secret meetings by letter. Once the Germans learned this, they simply sent letters to suspected French agents announcing when and where the next Résistance meeting was taking place.

And when Frenchmen showed up for the fake meeting, they were arrested!

Now here's a different spy-catching strategy: when FBI agent Robert Hanssen was suspected of selling American secrets, the first thing his bosses did was *promote* him to a better job.

Were they insane? No, but that's a good question. The idea was that promoting Hanssen would make the double agent *less* suspicious. I mean, why would the FBI promote someone it didn't trust? And this also made it easier for other FBI agents to track his movements.

In Hanssen's case, once the FBI had the needed proof, they arrested him. And it's no picnic for any spy to be *captured* (unless the spy was actually caught AT a picnic). But while soggy potato salad is bad, SMERSH was worse. That was the name of the spy-catching branch of the old Russian spy agency known as the KGB. Its name came from *Smyert Shpionam*, which means "death to spies." Yikes!

Although a caught spy might be executed, good manners still sometimes existed. After World War I broke out, the British MI5 caught a German spy named Carl Lody. But even though Lody was an enemy agent, the British still respected his brilliance and bravery. As Lody waited for his execution, he asked the British officer in charge of his firing squad, "I suppose you will not shake hands with a spy?"

The officer replied, "No, but I will shake hands with a brave man." And the two men shook hands.

VOCABULARY!

Exfiltration is the opposite of infiltration. It's what a spy does when he tries to sneak *out* of a country.

THE SCARIEST SPOT IN RUSSIA

The KGB was a scary spy agency. There was even a knock-knock joke about how scary it was.

"Knock knock!"

"Who's there?"

"The KGB."

"The KGB wh—"

"Silence! *Nobody* questions the KGB!"

KGB headquarters were in a massive Moscow building called Lubyanka. And it doubled as a prison for spies. How bad was Lubyanka? The people who worked there were nicknamed "bone crushers." And according to prisoners, Lubyanka was kept as silent as possible. Guards did not speak, but communicated instead by clicking their tongues.

The idea was that all that tongue clicking would be so eerie, it would freak prisoners out. And it did!

For anyone imprisoned in Lubyanka, the greatest hope was to be shipped out to a work camp in Siberia. Although that may not sound so great, it definitely beat the other alternatives: torture or death.

And that's why the Russians liked to tell this joke:

Q. What's the tallest building in Moscow?

A. Lubyanka. You can see Siberia from its basement!

Strangely, if you visit the most-feared spot in Russia today, you can take a tour. In fact, you can even visit the cellar (a.k.a. the Cell), where spies were executed. (As for me, I'll be waiting outside.)

But most agencies would rather catch and interrogate a spy than assassinate one. As far as I know, the strangest thing a captured spy ever had to keep secret during an interrogation was a *poem*. That's because British agents who needed to translate top secret codes were once given poems with the code "key" hidden within them.

And so captured agents faced interrogations about their poetry!

Interrogator: We have ways of making you recite poetry.

Spy: I'll **NEVER** reveal my poem to you!

Interrogator (*swinging a large wet noodle*): Don't make me use this.

Spy: Not the noodle! Okay, okay: *"The itsy-bitsy spider went up the water spout . . ."*

Mean Interrogator (*sitting down*): Ooh, I love this one.

IF YOU'RE CAUGHT

If you allow yourself to be captured by enemy agents, remember to use a good alibi. That's why you should never start spying without already having an excuse prepared. The CIA calls this "plausible denial." When a U.S. spy plane (called the U-2) was shot down over Russia, the CIA had its plausible denial ready: *That wasn't a spy plane, that was an unarmed plane monitoring the weather. So thanks a lot for shooting down our harmless science project, you jerks!*[2]

---

2. Unfortunately, the pilot then confessed to being a spy, which sort of ruined the denial.

Here's my favorite "plausible denial" story of all time! In 1980, there was a revolution in Iran. During that time, the U.S. embassy in Iran was taken over and the Americans inside were held hostage while mobs of people shouting "Death to America!" filled the streets.

There were also Americans trapped *outside* the embassy, including a group of six who were holed up in a Canadian diplomat's home. Since ALL Americans were suspected of being spies, getting these six out of Iran was a huge safety concern.

So a CIA agent named Antonio Mendez invented a fake movie company called "Studio Six Productions." And his fake studio took out ads for a fake science-fiction film called *Argo*. It even had a cheesy slogan: "Studio Six Productions presents *Argo*: A cosmic conflagration!"

The six stranded Americans were given disguises. They were going to pose as actors and Hollywood types working on the *Argo* movie. One older American diplomat was given a blow-dried hairstyle. He also had on tight pants, a topcoat that he wore like a cape, and a blue silk shirt unbuttoned down the front and showing a gold chain and medallion!

In short, the outfits were so outrageous, this plan HAD to work. And it did! The six "film" people managed to persuade the Iranians that they weren't spies, and they got safely out of the country.

Now dig this: since there was no need for it to exist anymore, Studio Six Productions was dismantled. But during the weeks it had existed, the fake studio had received over two dozen scripts for movies, including one by a young Steven Spielberg!

Of course, it's unlikely that you'll need a plan as complex as the Studio Six one. Let me think of a more likely scenario that you might have to deal with. Got it!

Accusation: You were picking your nose.

Plausible Denial: A bug flew up your nose, and you were trying to save its life.

Of course, as a spy, your greatest danger isn't a bug up your nose; it's being captured. You're committing crimes with a secret identity, and your employer doesn't want to admit that you exist. Not good! In Russia, they once had a special execution for enemy spies called *vyshaya mera*.[3] Luckily, many nations are now more humane to captured agents. This is partly because torture doesn't get anyone good information. Think about it: if someone were threatening you with a hedge-trimmer, you'd say ANYTHING to keep it away from you!

But there are OTHER mean things that interrogators might try, including

- 👁 sleep deprivation
- 👁 loud noises
- 👁 bright lights
- 👁 bribes
- 👁 brainwashing
- 👁 hypnosis
- 👁 annoying music.

Yes, interrogators have been known to play the theme songs from *Sesame Street* and *Barney* over and over and over again to wear down a captured spy. (Seriously.)

Of course, you won't need to use these interrogation techniques, because you have THIS book. Simply read aloud from it to the captured spy. *That* will get results!

---

3. The spy was shot in the back of the head with a huge gun. This makes identifying the person by his face impossible.

THE INTERROGATION: SPOTTING A SPY-ER WHO'S A LIAR

It's easy to tell the truth. That's one reason why most people tell the truth most of the time. It's the comfortable thing to do! So during an interrogation, these are signs that a suspect is probably telling the truth:

1. Answers questions completely and directly.
2. Acts attentive and interested.
3. Answers quickly.
4. Gives consistent answers that don't conflict with each other or require explanations.

Ah, but when a person lies, everything changes! Now our suspect has to keep at least TWO things in mind at once: the LIE and the TRUTH. This creates conflict, and it makes a person feel UNcomfortable. And if someone is uncomfortable, you can spot it.

So before you start your interview, all you need is a clipboard, some paper, and a pen. As your interview starts, simply watch for any of the following signs. Every time you observe one of the signs, mark a little dot on your clipboard. These dots will help you see patterns of lying.

If you have your questions written out beforehand, mark the dots next to the question being asked. This helps locate specific topics where lies happen.[4] And if this seems like a lot of stuff to look out for, have someone ELSE ask the questions. Then you can just keep track of the dots! Oh, and try not to sit across the table from the person you're questioning. It's better to be on the same side of the table and turn towards him so you can see his entire body.

BODY POSITION: Whether seated or standing, everyone has an "anchor point." This is a spot where the body weight rests. And a liar will shift anchor points a lot! If seated, he may lean on one elbow and then shift to another one. Standing? He may keep switching his weight from foot to foot. Or his legs may bounce and twitch so fast, neither one is being used as an anchor point for very long.

BODY LANGUAGE: Lots of grooming gestures can be a tip-off. Is the person adjusting her glasses, touching her hair, or picking at her

---

4. This technique is taken from a method that a CIA interrogator created. It's called Tactical Behavior Assessment, or TBA.

fingernails? Is she putting the items around her (like pens or notebooks) in neat little rows? A liar might have lots of body language. So look for touching, rubbing, or tugging on the ears, nose, and eyes, as well as readjusting her clothes.[5]

EYES: It's possible to lie with normal eye contact. But if the person can't look *away* from you OR can't look *at* you, then she MAY be lying. And liars really DO blink more than normal!

VOICE: It is stressful to lie, so a liar's voice tends to go higher than normal. Liars also tend to talk fast. However, if the liar has to invent a lie on the spot, he will slow way down and look upwards as he searches for the best story.

If the person is *really* feeling the stress, there may be stuttering and a lot of pauses and mumbling. Liars also use "filler words" like *er, um, duh, uh,* or *help me, I'm a big fat liar.*

UH, WELL, LET ME SEE . . .

---

5. A *really* defensive liar may freeze up and have fewer hand gestures than usual. Her hands may go into her pockets and never come out, or she may cross her legs and arms and stay in that posture.

FAKE SMILES AND LAUGHING: It isn't THAT hard to spot a fake smile, because liars only smile with their *mouth*.

What we mean is that a true smile affects the *whole face*, so that the corners of the eyes will "crinkle" up. If a person has a thin-lipped, clenched-teeth smile that doesn't crinkle the eyes, it's probably a fake.

And a laugh is only real if the person closes his eyes as he laughs. If your suspect starts laughing but is watching you with open eyes when he does, it's as fake as a three-dollar bill.

WORD USE: A liar is trying to convince you, and he'll use phrases like *"To tell the truth," "Really," "Honestly," "Actually," "No kidding," "Seriously,"* more than usual. Be sure to mark a dot for any version of these.

- 👁 *"Frankly . . ."*
- 👁 *"To the best of my knowledge . . ."*
- 👁 *"Trust me."*
- 👁 *"Why would I lie?"*
- 👁 *"I swear."*
- 👁 *"You can ask anyone!"*
- 👁 *". . . as I said before . . ."*

👁 *"How dare you ask me that!"* (Or *"I can't believe you're asking me that question."*)

👁 *"How long is this going to take?"*

A person who ends statements with *"All right?"* or *"Don't you agree?"* or *"You know what I'm talking about?"* or other questions that try to get *you* to agree to what it was she said is also possibly lying.

Finally, a person who is lying uses "contractions" less and emphasizes denials. For example, instead of saying *"I didn't do it,"* she will say *"I did NOT do it."*

I SWEAR I DID NOT EAT THE PICKLE SANDWICH!

As you make your dots, remember that you're looking for **PATTERNS**. So if you ask a question and your suspect shifts in his seat, gives a fake laugh, and says, *"Why would you ask me that question?"* you're probably on to something.

Even so, there will rarely be times when you can be 100 percent sure that someone is guilty. An innocent person who is anxious might fidget. So look for **LOTS** of dots, not just a few.

THE QUESTIONS!

You might begin by asking your suspect a nonthreatening question, something like "*What was the first day at school like?*" or another vivid memory. There's no reason for the person to lie, so pay close attention to the way this person tells the TRUTH.

As you shift to your real questions, think: Is the person providing the same number of details that he did before? And the way you phrase your questions is also important. Don't ask specific, confrontational questions like:

Are you a spy?

When did you become evil?

Why did you steal the polka-dotted laptop?

Instead, try indirect LEADING questions. These might lead the person to actually talk about the subject. For example,

Why do you think you're in this situation?

Is there any reason we'd find your fingerprints on the polka-dotted laptop?

Weren't you worried that someone might notice the polka-dotted laptop was gone?

The key is to get your suspect to TALK. The more a person talks, the more likely he is to feel like getting that secret off his chest.

And if you had your suspect tell a story, try this. After the suspect finishes, have him describe everything that happened in reverse! A liar is going to have a VERY hard time doing this, but an honest person can. In fact, while telling the story backwards, the story may gain relevant details!

TELLING THE TRUTH: ONCE YOU CAN FAKE THAT, YOU'VE GOT IT MADE!

Remember, all of these techniques can also be used on YOU. But while intelligence experts often give classes on how to detect lies, they almost *never* give classes on how to lie. That's because it just doesn't work. Lie detectors are the worst liars around! So it turns out that knowing what to look for doesn't help you become a better liar yourself!

I can give you a few weak tips about things to try if you're being interrogated.

Answering questions with questions: "Before I tell you about my mission, what's your favorite color?"

Claiming ignorance: "Wow, how weird that I forgot my own name!"

Giving outrageously general answers: "My favorite color? Rainbow."

Changing the topic: "I guess I'm sitting here today because I like pickles. In fact, canning pickles is one of my favorite hobbies. I am especially interested in sweet pickles, and so forth."

AVOID YOUR MOTHER TONGUE!

Chinese spy Larry Wu-Tai Chin (p. 252) took—and passed—lie detector tests even though he was lying. But Chin took these tests in English, and he said he passed the lie detector because it's easier to lie in a foreign language.

The fact is that a professional interviewer will find a way to get the truth out of you. In Israel, there was recently a murder case. The police had a suspect, but he said he had no memory of any crime.

A police officer then went to the hospital and borrowed an ECG machine, which measures heart rate. He also brought some electrodes and ECG printouts. The officer set the machine up in an interview room, along with a laptop computer. The suspect was brought in and agreed to be hooked up to the "memory machine."

The suspect allowed electrodes to be attached to his head, with other dummy wires leading to the laptop. The police then began the interview. When the suspect again denied any memory of the murder, the officer said, "You're lying! The exam shows that you DO remember!"

The suspect was then shown the ECG printout from the hospital. Faced with the "evidence," the suspect confessed to the murder! The police later explained to him that there is no such thing as a "memory machine." (This probably did not make him very happy.)

Of course, there ARE real lie-detector machines. Traditional lie detectors measure a person's heart rate and breathing. One recent lie detector uses a laser pointer. This is aimed at a person's throat, where it measures the blood flow to the brain. More blood?—more lies! And there is also a lie-detecting camera that detects temperature changes in a person's face. A person who is lying has a heat increase in the inside corner of her eyes!

NOW WHAT?

After a spy is caught and interrogated, what do you do with him? In the old days, a captured spy might be "terminated with extreme prejudice." But today, we know it's wrong to be prejudiced, so we just kill them.

Ha! Just kidding. You could try to imprison the spy, but I'm guessing that your closet will get kind of cramped. Maybe your best option is to try to "flip" the captured spy. This does not refer to martial arts; flipping (or "turning") a spy means that you get them to switch over to YOUR side and become a double agent.

Of course, nobody trusts a double agent. Since the spy is not loyal to his original employers, that makes him a traitor. And a traitor is the LAST person you should trust!

As masters of deception, double agents all have one thing in common. When one of them gets caught, she'll claim that she was trying to become a TRIPLE agent. That is, the spy will admit to working for the other side, but only to fool the enemy. She was *secretly* loyal to your side all along!

Right.

But trying to flip a spy is still a good way to go. Because if you threaten or mistreat your captured spy, she will definitely backstab you at the first chance! So take a more positive approach. Like my granny always said, "You catch more spies with honey than with vinegar."

Let's learn from intelligence agent Jim Soiles. He needed information from a former terrorist named Samir. Although Samir had recently been arrested, he refused to talk or cooperate in any way.

Agent Soiles decided it was time for some *honey*. He knew where Samir was from, so the agent went to a specialty deli that made food from that region. Agent Soiles then ordered two lunches to go and brought them back to the prison.

Once there, Soiles had Samir brought to a visiting room. Neither man said anything. Soiles then set both lunches on a table and silently ate one of them. Samir just watched him. Finally, Soiles threw the other lunch in the trash and left, still without having said a word.

The next day, Soiles did the exact same thing. And the next day. And the next day! For a whole month, neither man said anything while Soiles enjoyed a delicious lunch and threw the other lunch away. But FINALLY, one day as Soiles sat down to eat, Samir said, "What do you want?"

Not only did Samir eat lunch that day, but Soiles and Samir have been working together ever since!

This shows that patience pays off in intelligence work. (It also shows that prison food is probably pretty lousy.) Anyway, since most spies get paid for their work, another approach for flipping a spy might be to offer a captured spy more money than his employer pays. Other possibilities include giving the spy a chance for revenge or a solution to a problem he has.

One mean way to get a captured agent to cooperate is called "false flag deception." Here, the recruited spy is told that he will be working for a certain agency or country when he is *actually* working for an entirely different one! In other words, Russian spies might pretend to be American agents, thus tricking the flipped spy.

But the most common dirty trick is just to threaten a captured spy, often with blackmail. However, many agents (like me!) have such innocent lives, it doesn't matter if their enemies take secret photographs of it.

The Best-Dressed
AGENTS

Throughout history, important people have hired bodyguards to protect their . . . bodies. Usually, these guards stayed right by the person they were protecting to scare away would-be assassins.

Take the Praetorian Guard of ancient Rome, for instance. Assigned to keep the emperor safe, these warriors stood openly and proudly behind their leader, gleaming armor and sharpened weapons at the ready. The Praetorians made

PRAETORIAN GUARD
WE'VE GOT YOUR BACK!

up the most bloodthirsty, toughest bodyguards you could imagine! How awesome were they? Well, the Praetorian Guard itself was responsible for the deaths or disappearances of ten different Roman emperors!

Yep—the bodyguards often KILLED the guys they were supposed to be protecting. So maybe having the guards onstage wasn't such a good idea after all. Clearly, these Praetorians wanted more attention than was healthy!

Maybe this explains why the Secret Service is in charge of protecting the President of the United States of America. (Note the key word: SECRET.) They're *supposed* to keep a low profile! But while you might not notice them, Secret Service agents don't just stand around by the president's side. They keep busy. After all, an average of about 30 people each year try to ram the White House gates with cars, or climb over the fence that surrounds it, or get on the grounds some other way. The fact that none of these attempts work tells us how effective these agents are.

HIT THEM WITH YOUR BEST SHOT

When the president is on the move, agents are stationed as snipers along his travel route. Their job is to keep an eye on the crowd and be ready to "pick off" would-be assassins. These agent snipers are pretty amazing shots. They are tested monthly on being able to hit targets 1,000 yards away.

But one of the greatest challenges that Secret Service agents face is the president himself! Over the years, presidents have often gotten tired of having bodyguards constantly around them, so sometimes they make a break for it. For instance, President Gerald Ford (term 1974–77) was a terrific skier. He would often get off a chair lift and go tearing down the mountain, taunting the agents, who were eating his snow. (Good thing the Praetorian Guard wasn't around. They probably would have fired an arrow through Ford's ski goggles.)

To deal with the runaway president, his Secret Service agents assigned the best skier on the force to President

Ford. This agent was so world class, he'd get in front of Ford and then turn around and ski BACKWARDS down the mountain while Ford tried to keep up!

And *then* he'd shoot an arrow through Ford's ski-goggles. (Kidding!)

The Secret Service is also in charge of guarding the vice president. This is usually a little easier, as the v.p. isn't as popular a target for assassination. In fact, when George H. W. Bush was vice president (1981–89), Agent William Albracht was posted to be the overnight guard at Bush's home. The agent was jokingly instructed that it was the responsibility of the house's cooks to bake cookies for the next day. And it was the responsibility of Secret Service agents to FIND those cookies!

Albracht laughed, but by 3 a.m., he was getting hungry. He went into the kitchen to do some reconnaissance. No cookies. Suddenly, there was a voice behind him!

"Hey, anything in there good to eat?" It was George Bush! And so the Secret Service agent and the Vice President of the United States combined forces to find the hidden cookies. *Mission accomplished.* Bush went back to bed with a glass of milk and a stack of chocolate chip cookies. And as for the Secret Service agent, he enjoyed the sweet taste of victory.

★ *Keeping Secrets Is Easy Underwater:* The submarine fleet of the U.S. Navy is known as the *Silent Service.*

It used to be a lot easier to get into the White House. Since the president is chosen BY the people, the idea was that the president should be available TO the people. And that's why the first American presidents didn't have ANY bodyguards at all.

This led to some awkward moments. When the White House was first built, a crazed man wandered into the building, intent on killing President John Adams. This wasn't a security breakdown. There WAS no security, and the White House was open to the public! Since Adams didn't have any bodyguards to call for help, he did something sensible: the president invited the crazed man into his office and talked to him calmly.

Problem solved! (Temporarily.)

By the time Abraham Lincoln took office, he received so many death threats that he *had* to have a bodyguard. So police officers working in shifts were assigned to protect Lincoln. But these early bodyguards didn't take their jobs very seriously. Take Officer John Parker. He was on duty in 1865, the night Lincoln went to a play at Ford's Theater. And when John Wilkes Booth shot President Lincoln in the back of the head, Parker was down the street in a saloon, having a drink.

Amazingly, Lincoln's death failed to teach a lesson about presidential security. It took 36 more years and two more presidential assassinations before the Secret Service was **FINALLY** given the responsibility for protecting the president.

The Secret Service had already been around for years, but its main job had been to catch "counterfeiters" who made fake money. (Many states minted their own cash back then, and about a third of all the money in circulation was counterfeit.)

Once the Secret Service was in charge of presidential security, its agents immediately tried to stop the practice of allowing visitors to freely roam the White House. But this policy wouldn't changed until the 1940s. But enough history. It's time for a test!

1. Imagine that you're in the Secret Service. You've had training in firearms, spotting suspicious people in crowds, evasive driving, and many other awesome things. But during your training, which of the following lessons was **MOST** important?
   a. Learning how to take a bullet for the president.
   b. Learning not to flinch at the sound of gunfire.
   c. Learning how to defuse a stink bomb.

Answer below![1]

---

1. b. *Learning not to flinch at the sound of gunfire.* With proper safeguards, no agent should have to "take a bullet." (And contrary to popular belief, stink bombs are ineffective assassination weapons!)

2. True or False? Secret Service agents wear sunglasses to look cool. While this is nice, it also makes it easy to spot the agents.

Answer below![2]

3. When people threaten the life of the president, which of these types of messages do you think most people use for their threats?

   a. Phone call

   b. Email

   c. IM

   d. Video

   e. Snail mail

Answer below![3]

4. All presidents receive threats, and lots of them. But when a certain president took office, the rate of presidential threats increased 400 percent. Who was this president?

Answer below.[4]

5. Secret Service agents refer to would-be assassins as

   a. barmy.

---

2. *False* and *false!* Glasses are worn for eye protection and also so that people cannot see where the agents are looking. But there are also plainclothes agents without shades or earpieces, walking around the White House or wherever the president is located.

3. e. *Snail mail.* Surprised? Me too, but apparently, letter writers think the president will actually read a real letter.

4. *Barack Obama.* Being the first black president meant that he was a target for racists, and the Secret Service had to be on high alert at all times.

b. jackals.

c. sadly misguided individuals.

Answer below![5]

If you got all of these answers right, you might consider a career in the Secret Service. Oh, and have you guessed why Secret Service agents are the best dressed of all agents? Just think of all the formal dinners, galas, and balls that the president and his family have to attend. That means the bodyguards protecting the president have to be in their best formal wear a lot of the time. I mean, have you ever seen an agent in a T-shirt and flip-flops at a presidential speech?

But not all Secret Service agents are dressed in suits and wearing sunglasses. Whenever the president makes a public appearance, there are a number of agents in plainclothes, moving through the crowd. Yes, they are *secret* Secret Service agents. But whatever their outfit might be, you just know that all of the agents want to have that little microphone in their shirtsleeves. These are excellent for communicating with other officers—and they have other uses, too!

5. b. *Jackals.*

FAMOUS (& Infamous) SPIES

A spy goal is to be invisible, secret, and otherwise unnoticed. That means a good agent is like an *anti*-celebrity! So, does this mean that famous spies are actually losers? I'm not sure. Maybe I need to ask an expert, like . . .

THE SPY WHO'D SCHOOL YOU

Elsbeth Schragmüller (1887–1940) was a German who became the dean of a school for spies that she founded. And not only did she have that going for her, but Schragmüller also had two cool nicknames: "Tiger Eyes" and "Fräulein Doktor."

When World War I began, Schragmüller volunteered for service to Germany. Fräulein Doktor's intelligence and savvy led her to lead a school for spies. Much of this school's activities are still shrouded in secrecy. But supposedly, to make sure the students at the espionage school didn't know each other's identities, Schragmüller had them all wear masks! And to graduate, the spy students had to undertake an actual (but safe) mission that involved deception, guts, and intelligence.

REPORT CARD

Deception: B+ — Good, but signs of honesty still exist.

Code Breaking: A — Highest marks in class!

Breaking & Entering: C+ — Excellent at breaking, so-so at entering.

Garrote defense: D — Student can't tell difference between guitar and piano wire.

WOODEN LEG? WHAT WOODEN LEG?

Virginia Hall (1906–1982) was a one-legged spy for the Allies in World War II. And she may have been the best there was. German intelligence said, "She is the most dangerous of all Allied spies. We must find and destroy her."

Hall never intended to be a spy, though! She was working for the U.S. State Department when she was accidentally shot in a hunting accident. Hall's left leg had to be amputated and replaced with a wooden one. Forced to quit her job, Hall chose to become a journalist. Her intelligence and bravery led British agents to recruit her when World War II broke out.

As a spy, Hall worked with the French Resistance. She spent almost three years in occupied France. During that time, she narrowly escaped capture by the Nazis' secret police force, the Gestapo. Given her limp and accent, this was especially remarkable!

In addition to being praised for her courage, Hall got a cool nickname—"Agent Heckler." She showed her humor by also giving her artificial leg its own code name: Cuthbert. As a joke, Virginia Hall once told her boss that she hoped "Cuthbert" wouldn't give her any trouble as she escaped on foot from France to Spain.

Not getting the joke, the spymaster's response was, "If Cuthbert [is] troublesome, eliminate him."

THE WORLD'S GREATEST LOVER WAS A SPY!

Giovanni Casanova (1725–1798) was a legendary ladies' man. And for years, he was also a secret agent in France and Italy. Casanova seemed to enjoy his spy work, saying, "I did not hesitate to deceive nitwits and scoundrels and fools."

TOO HONEST FOR HIS OWN GOOD

Nathan Hale (1755–1776) was the first American spy. Which is ridiculous, because by now YOU have had more military training than he did! Before joining the revolutionaries, Hale was a schoolteacher. In 1776, after learning that George Washington supported spying, Hale volunteered to be an agent, even though the teacher had NO background in intelligence. And there were important factors working against Hale. For instance, he was really tall and he had a big scar on his face. In short, Hale stuck out!

But Hale *was* brave. He managed to sneak into the British encampment in Manhattan. Then he managed to get caught after a few days. Since Hale wasn't a professional spy, he believed that honesty was the best policy. MISTAKE! He *admitted* to being a spy. And so the commander of the British forces ordered Hale's execution. (This was a rip-off, as there was no trial.) Before he was hanged, Hale reportedly said, "I only regret that I have but one life to lose for my country." I think we all agree those are pretty awesome last words.

REMINDER: WHAT NOT TO DO

Grim Man: Are you a spy?

Young Person (enthusiastically): YES! How'd you know?

WHO ARE WE WORKING FOR?

The CIA defends the U.S. from its enemies. But every now and then, someone suggests that its spies do industrial/commercial espionage for American corporations. To that, one CIA agent said, "I'm prepared to give my life for my country, but not for a company."

ORGANIZED CHAOS

In the very silly TV show and movie *Get Smart*, super-agent Maxwell Smart is assigned to stop the evil plots of an international organization known as **KAOS.** But it turns out that the KAOS name wasn't as goofy as the show's writers believed. The CIA actually started something called Operation CHAOS (pronounced KAY-oss) in 1967. CHAOS was created to watch American war protesters to see if they had support from other governments.

After tracking thousands of people for years, CHAOS reached a startling conclusion: some people just don't like wars!

BRITISH SPIES LIKE TO WRITE!

Daniel Defoe (ca. 1660–1731) wrote the famous survival story *Robinson Crusoe*. He was also a troublemaker who ended up being thrown into jail a few times. But because Defoe was extremely smart, had a terrific memory, and observed EVERYTHING, he was recruited by the British government to be a spy.

Defoe was so good at spying, he ended up in charge of a spy network in England that he created himself. (For this, he was called "the father of the British secret service.") Then Defoe got so caught up in the double-crossing world of espionage, it got to the point where he would befriend and then betray almost *anyone*.

Well, you know what they say: never trust a writer!

Roald Dahl (1916–1990) grew up around secrets. In fact, he ate them! Before he became the author of classics like *Charlie and the Chocolate Factory, The Witches,* and *James and the Giant Peach*, Dahl went to school near the headquarters for the Cadbury candy company. There, Dahl and his fellow students were used as taste-testers for newly invented sweets. This gave Dahl a lifelong interest in candy and high security. (See p. 287 to see what I mean.) And as an adult, Dahl was a spy for the British government during World War II.

FLYING CARS RULE

Dahl also wrote a children's book about a flying car called *Chitty Chitty Bang Bang* in 1964. At first, I didn't see why, but then I realized that *Chitty Chitty Bang Bang* can take aerial reconnaissance photos!

Ian Fleming (1908–1964) joined British Intelligence in 1939, where he showed himself to be an imaginative agent who was good at plotting dangerous missions. Fleming's abilities led him to directing a group of commandos that stole enemy papers and infiltrated Nazi spy agencies. Not only that, but Fleming carried around a fountain pen with a tear-gas canister inside it! (Or at least that's what he said.)

After the war, Fleming began writing fictional plots for his invented super-spy, James Bond. He partly got the idea for Bond after meeting a super-smooth Serbian spy named Dusan Popov (see p. 258).

As you already know, James Bond's official name was Agent 007, which means he has a "license to kill." It turns out that these licenses are very hard to get; I've tried and tried, and the best I've been able to come up with is a "permit to kick shins." (CIA director William Webster used to sign his name as "0014" to double his badness.)

Another thing you may have noticed is how Bond's boss at the MI6 office is called "M." This comes from a real tradition; the first head of the MI6 was only called "C," and later directors have also been known by that initial. As it turns out, the first director's name was Sir Mansfield Cumming. He was pretty cool, and not just because he had a wooden leg.

THE OVERACHIEVER

Amy Elizabeth Brousse (1910–1963) may have been one of the greatest spies of all time. But what made her so good? She was smart—VERY smart. Brousse wrote a novel at the age of eleven! And she was also beautiful. This was helpful because her looks helped Amy trick other experienced spies into revealing some very important things.

Born an American, Amy later married a British diplomat and soon became a member of that country's intelligence service. After World War II began, Amy began working in Washington, D.C., under the cover of being a reporter. Her actual assignment: find the secret codes that Italy was using. (Italy was allied with the Nazis.)

An Italian diplomat named Alberto Lais was in Washington, D.C., then. Not only had Lais read Amy's childhood novel, he'd also met her while she was still a teenager. So Amy reintroduced herself to the Italian. And from him, she got more secrets than anyone would have thought possible—including word of Italy's secret plans to sabotage the U.S. Navy![1]

But that's not why Amy is famous.

After Germany invaded France, the Nazis set up an organization called the Vichy government to rule the French. So Amy, still pretending to be a reporter, contacted the press officer for the Vichy government. This man, Charles Brousse, fell in love with Amy. This allowed Amy to admit to being a spy—and Charles didn't care! He gave her secret letters, files, and telegrams.

But what Amy REALLY wanted were the Vichy government's secret codes.

That's where Brousse drew the line. These codes were in a locked room in the embassy, inside a locked safe! And at night, the locked codes were guarded by a watchman with a mean dog.

To solve these difficulties, Amy teamed up with American agents, who enlisted a safecracker for her. This led to a daring plan:

---

1. After getting all of the Italian's intelligence, Amy reported Lais to the FBI and he was deported.

1. Brousse (who was married) would tell the watchman that he needed a place to meet a woman he was having a secret affair with. (The watchman wasn't suspicious because the French love this kind of thing.) So Brousse would bribe the watchman to look the other way when he came into the embassy late at night with Amy.

2. Amy would then slip drugs into a glass of champagne and give it to the watchman. Next, they would also give the dog some drugged food.

3. Then they would let the safecracker into the embassy. He would break into the locked room and into the locked safe. After photographing the codebooks, the books would be returned to their location.

And the plan almost worked! The guard drank his champagne. *Zzzz*. The dog ate his drugged dog food. *Zzzz*. But the safecracker couldn't get the safe open in time!

★ *You Are Getting Sleepy:* The CIA called its dog tranquilizers "Puppy Chow."

It actually took TWO more tries like this before Amy got into the safe and the codes were photographed and safely returned. Mission accomplished! After that, Amy returned to England, where she apparently volunteered to serve as an assassin. (Man, where did she come from?)

When asked if she was ever ashamed of the work she did in the war, Amy said, "Not in the least. My superiors told me that the results of my work saved thousands of British and American lives. . . . Wars are not won by respectable methods."

After the war, Amy's husband died, Brousse and his wife divorced, and then Brousse and Amy got married. They moved into a castle in France and lived together until Amy's death in 1963. As for Brousse, he died 10 years later when he was electrocuted by his electric blanket.

Imagine that! He survived the Nazis but was killed by his own blanket.

ISRAEL'S GREATEST SPY?

Eli Cohen (1924–1965) may have been the most famous Mossad (p. 42) agent ever. He was an Israeli mole who snuck into an extremely high-ranking job with the government of one of Israel's biggest enemies, Syria. Cohen pretended to be a wealthy Arab named Asmin Tsa-bet and became friends with Syrian president Amin al-Hafez! Wow—friends with the president of an enemy nation!

Cohen's exploits were the stuff of legend. One story suggests that he persuaded the Syrians to plant eucalyptus trees in front of some secret bunkers they were building. Cohen explained that the shade would keep the soldiers more comfortable in the desert heat. When war between Syria and Israel later broke out, Cohen then told the Israeli air force to bomb anywhere they saw eucalyptus trees!

For two years, Cohen sent secret information to Israel using a radio transmitter before he was caught and convicted by the Syrians. (Cohen was hanged in a public square. It was televised.)

Although Cohen was caught, a former Mossad chief once said, "What if I were to tell you that there are many Eli Cohens? And that if they are successful, you will never hear of them?"

It makes you wonder!

ONE OF THE CIA'S FOUNDING FATHERS

William J. "Wild Bill" Donovan (1883–1959) helped found the spy agency that later became the CIA. It was called the Office of Strategic Services (OSS), but before it was created, Wild Bill had some persuading to do. It turned out that a lot of American officials just did NOT want an American spy agency.

For example, Ruth Shipley was the head of passports for government employees. She insisted on stamping a big "OSS" on the passport of any OSS employee. Not helpful! That would be like stamping "CIA" on the passports of American spies today—it sort of blows their cover.

To make his case for the OSS, Wild Bill visited the White House to demonstrate to President Franklin D. Roosevelt how effective U.S. spies could be. While the president was on the phone in the Oval Office, Donovan fired ten shots from a spy pistol into a bag of sand. Then Wild Bill placed the smoking gun on the president's desk. And Roosevelt hadn't heard a single shot!

One of my favorite Donovan stories came about during World War II. It was then that he okayed a stink weapon nicknamed "Who, Me?" It was just a metal tube with a screw cap, but the tube was filled with a liquid that smelled like the worst poop you can imagine. The idea was to give Chinese children thousands of the tubes. Then the kids would secretly spray it on the uniforms of Japanese officers. And the officers would freak out at the stinkiness!

While the idea had a few problems, Wild Bill didn't mind. That's because his working motto was "Go ahead and try it." I think this should be YOUR motto too. (If you don't know if you like it, just go ahead and try it for a while.)

THE 12 TYPES
of Spy Screw-Ups

As you know, spies are very important people. After all, they can help win wars that would have been lost without them. But spies can also LOSE battles that would have been won!

So, remember, for every epic spy failure there is also an epic WIN! And that win is for the enemy side. But maybe I shouldn't make such a big deal about failures. I mean, it's only normal for people to make mistakes. Even me!

For example, you know that *simple* plans are the best plans. Recently, I was assigned to follow a foreign agent. This spy was using an ice cream truck as a cover for his operation.

To keep things simple, I reviewed and memorized the information we had on this ice cream mastermind. Then I imagined myself following the agent without him noticing me. (We spies call this "positive visualization" or "pretending.") Finally, I have a little superstition where I always have tea and crumpets before going out on a job. As you can see, I kept it simple!

By the time I got to where my target was supposed to be, he was long gone. Rats! But at least once I did *something* right just to get my spy job in the first place. When I first applied, I was part of a group of other spy wannabes. All of us were given sealed envelopes with our names on them. We were told to take these and go up to the sixth floor. As the group left, I was overcome with curiosity. What was in MY envelope?

I slyly ducked into an empty office and managed to open the envelope without breaking the seal. It had a single piece of paper inside it, which read: "Nice work. You're hired! Report to Human Resources on the tenth floor."

Yes! And I'm trying to remind myself of how smart I am as I wonder where that ice cream truck is. And I'm also thinking about the many different kinds of mistakes spies make. Here's some now!

1. AN ENEMY SPY IS SPOTTED! BUT THERE'S ONE PROBLEM . . .

In 1970, an informant in Vietnam told a CIA agent about an enemy spy. This spy was a woman who was selling secret U.S. military documents right on the street in Saigon!

The CIA agent looked into it and found the woman. She was disguised as a cookie seller on a street corner! Approaching her, the agent was surprised to find that the enemy agent was selling cookies wrapped in Navy documents stamped with the word "Confidential." Ah-HA!

An investigation began into what looked like a major spy ring. The cookie lady was code-named "Cookie Lady." (How brilliant was that?) CIA agents discovered that the Cookie Lady's papers were coming from the U.S. Naval office in Saigon. It turned out that a woman who worked at the office was *keeping* the confidential papers she was supposed to burn. Then the office worker was giving the papers to the Cookie Lady for her to wrap her cookies in. And NEITHER of the women could read English!

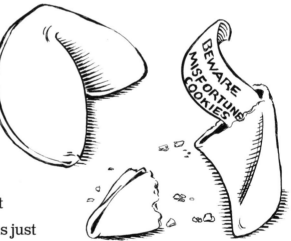

So it turned out that the Cookie Lady was just a cookie lady. (I guess you could say the whole conspiracy was half-baked.)

Moral: That's the way the cookie theory crumbles.

2. A SPY IS NOT SPOTTED! (AND THAT'S THE PROBLEM!)

A German spy named Baron August Schluga (1841–1917) pulled off the greatest victory in the history of spying. If anyone was going to do this, it was going to be the Baron. Schluga was so good that he pulled off tricks that his own side didn't understand. For example, Schluga's own spymaster didn't even know where the spy *lived*.

By 1914, Schluga (code named "Agent 17") was already a legend when he did something awe-inspiring. At the age of 73, Schluga somehow got his hands on France's entire military strategy! And it was real.

This was especially handy since France and Germany were about to go to war. Many experts believe this is the single most amazing feat any spy has ever accomplished. So how did Agent 17 do it? Good question! But Schluga kept his sources and methods secret to the day he died.

Moral: It's a secret.

3. THAT PERSON CAN'T BE A SPY. (RIGHT?)

When Syria got new Russian fighter-jets in 1966, its leaders were excited. These planes were WAY better than anything that Syria's archenemy, Israel, had!

But when a Syrian pilot then flew one of the new fighters *to* Israel and landed the plane there, it sort of took the fun out of the victory. And when it turned out that Israeli agents had persuaded the pilot to move to Israel, it was all very disappointing.

Moral: Trust nobody. Suspect everybody!

THREATENING BODY ODORS

In 1991, a CIA worker was called down to the agency's parking garage in Virginia. Bomb-sniffing dogs had picked up the scent of something dangerous in his car's trunk! As an armed squad stood by, the employee carefully opened his trunk and revealed the source of the dog's concern: his dirty workout clothes.

4. A SPY ISN'T SPOTTED UNTIL WAY TOO LATE (OR NOT AT ALL!).

Example A: Larry Wu-Tai Chin joined the CIA in 1952. He was prized for his ability to translate Chinese documents. Good catch! But Larry then sold U.S. secrets to the Chinese government for the next *40* years. He was a "mole"! This is the word used for spies who hide out in an organization.

Example B: In 1946, British intelligence appointed a man named Kim Philby. Why was it so bad that Philby was in charge of running spy operations against Russia? Because he was a *Russian* double agent! Philby wasn't found out for years, and he managed to successfully escape back to Russia in 1963.

Moral: Don't hire moles or double agents—unless they're REALLY qualified.

5. A SPY SELLS HIS CAMERA ON EBAY?

In 2008, a man bought a digital camera on eBay. After taking some pictures with it, he uploaded the photos to his computer. But what's this? The camera's memory card already HAD a bunch of images on it!

These pictures were of missiles, mean-looking bearded men holding rockets, and fingerprints of the mean-looking men who'd been holding the rockets. Oh, and there was also information about the encryption codes that the MI6 (see p. 293) uses for its computers.

It turned out that an MI6 officer on a terrorist detail had taken the photos and then neglected to wipe the memory card before selling the camera online.

Oops.

Moral: Cover your butt. And wipe the memory card.

6. A SPY SPENDS FIVE CENTS.

In 1953, a Russian spy named Reino Häyhänen spent a nickel somewhere in New York City. So what? Well, the spy accidentally used his secret hollow nickel! And this particular hollow nickel contained a coded espionage message on microfilm.

Oops!

The coin changed hands a few times, and then someone bought a newspaper with it. After the coin came apart, the surprised newspaper boy could see that it was a fake. Awesome! He reported the odd nickel and turned it over to the FBI. The following investigation became known as the Hollow Nickel Case. It took four years and resulted in the smashing of a Soviet spy ring and the arrest of an "art dealer" who turned out to be master Russian spy Rudolf Ivanovich Abel!

And all because someone spent the wrong nickel.

Moral: Carry exact change.

7. A CLEVER TRICK IS PLAYED!

Example A: During World War II, Spain sided with Germany. So when a "youth leader" from Spain came to

England in 1940 to learn about the Boy Scouts, it was a little suspicious. (And this youth leader really WAS a spy.)

The Brits were very kind to the Spaniard and even took him on a flight to Scotland. During this flight, the airplane was passed by endless squadrons of British fighters. The Spaniard was amazed at the hundreds of warplanes he saw! So when the Spanish spy made his secret report back to the Germans, he related that the British air force was very powerful. Clearly, invading Great Britain at that time was a BAD idea.

The only problem was that the British military was actually quite weak. The spy had only seen ONE squadron of British fighters . . . it just kept circling around and passing his plane over and over and over!

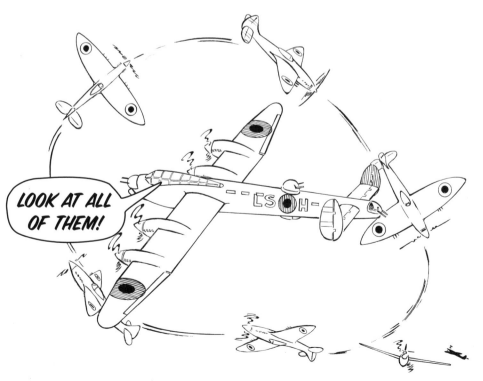

TRASH TALKING!

When a spy or agency scores a major victory, it's sometimes tempting to taunt the enemy. During World War II, the Germans caught or killed almost every British agent in Holland. After the Brits finally pulled all their agents from the country, they got a message from the Germans:

"Whenever you come to pay a visit . . . you will be received with the same care and result as all those you sent us before. So long."

No one saved the British reply, but my guess is that it was unprintable!

Example B: During World War I, Turkey fought the British in the Middle East. The Turkish forces had an excellent fortress in the town of Gaza. And when one of the Turkish fort's patrols chanced upon a British soldier, its soldiers fired at him. The frightened Brit dropped his backpack, and ran off in a panic!

Inside the blood-soaked backpack, the Turks learned they had *almost* caught a spy. It contained British attack plans and a codebook. Score! Using these, they found that the British were planning an attack on Gaza!

The Turks in Gaza got ready for the assault. So as you can imagine, they were totally surprised when the British attacked a DIFFERENT Turkish stronghold named

Beersheba instead. And in the following panic among the Turkish forces, the British took Beersheba, Jerusalem, *and* Gaza. Dang it!

It turned out that the whole thing had been a setup by the British. And the blood on the pack? It had been smeared on it before the Brit even went out on his patrol.

Moral: British agents are clever.

8. THOSE JERKS STOLE MY IDEA!

In the 1960s, a group of French and English researchers came up with a plan for a new jet called the Concorde. This aircraft would be able to fly faster than the speed of sound. Impressive! These researchers were flabbergasted when the Russians flew an EXACT copy of the Concorde in 1968, just before their original jet was ready to go. Talk about stealing someone else's glory! (The copycat jet was called the TY-144, but that didn't fool anyone.)

So how did the Russians do it? Simple. A spy named Sergei Fabiew had stolen the Concorde's plans and passed them along.

Moral: If a spy steals the plans for your plane, get revenge by canceling his frequent-flyer miles.

9. A SPY HAS GOOD INFORMATION ON SOMETHING REALLY IMPORTANT. AND NOBODY LISTENS!

Dusan Popov (1912–1981) was a real super-spy. He was a wealthy playboy and ladies' man who also worked undercover as a successful secret agent for Great Britain. Popov spoke several languages fluently and even developed his own recipe for invisible ink. He was a smooth operator! Popov was so impressive, writer Ian Fleming partly based James Bond on the famous spy.

In 1941, Popov learned of a secret Japanese plan to bomb almost the entire U.S. naval fleet at Pearl Harbor. And so he traveled to Washington, D.C., to warn the Americans! A meeting was arranged between Popov and J. Edgar Hoover, the head of the FBI. With a reputation like Popov's, you'd THINK that Hoover would have paid attention to the agent's warning. No dice. You see, there was one little problem with Popov that made Hoover suspicious.

Popov's secret spy code name was . . . "Tricycle"! And the director of the FBI couldn't imagine WHY a spy would have such an odd nickname. It was outrageous! Ludicrous! Suspicious!

So Popov was ignored, and Pearl Harbor caught almost everyone by complete surprise—everyone except J. Edgar Hoover.

Moral: Being a little paranoid is healthy. Being TOTALLY paranoid doesn't get you anywhere.

10. A SPY IS CAUGHT AND . . . HEY, WHERE'D HE GO?

George Blake was a high-level British intelligence agent. He was also spying for Russia from 1953 to 1961!

When Blake was caught, it was believed he had betrayed between 40 and 400 agents. That jerk! Blake was sentenced to prison, where he served five years. Then he managed to pull out a loose bar from his jail cell window, climb a down a rope ladder he had knitted himself, and escape. He left England and traveled to Moscow, where he conducted advanced classes for spies.

Oops.

Moral: Never let a captured spy knit. (You don't need a sweater that badly.)

11. A GREAT VICTORY TURNS INTO A DASHING DEFEAT!

During World War II, the British ambassador to Turkey left the top secret plans for the invasion of Europe in his personal safe. Bad idea! A spy named Ilyas Bazna, who was working for the Germans, made wax impressions of the ambassador's keys. With the copies he made, Bazna opened the ambassador's safe and photographed papers that gave away a number of Allied secrets, including the REAL plans to D-Day!

Bazna sold his fantastic intelligence to the German military for the equivalent of over a million dollars. And the Germans thought it was worth it! No one could believe how fantastic this information was!

No, seriously, the info was so good, the Germans eventually decided Bazna's information was fake and they never acted on it. *Oops!*

As for Bazna, he escaped to Argentina with his huge piles of cash. But when the time came to count his earnings, the spy had made a shocking discovery: the money the Germans had paid him was FAKE.

Double-oops!

Moral: You can sometimes trust a spy. But you can NEVER trust a Nazi.

12. NOBODY WILL EVER FIND THIS TOP SECRET STUFF!

The Russians once built a research station way far up into the Arctic. So, naturally, intelligence agents for the U.S. Navy were curious about what the Russians were doing. Was it submarine research? A new invention? What?

The Russians eventually abandoned their frosty and almost-impossible-to-get-to station. So the U.S. Navy created Operation Coldfeet to learn more about it! First, two agents were parachuted down to the station. They spent two days finding dozens of top secret documents and pieces of equipment. And on the third day, the agents left in an unusual way.

The Arctic location was too remote for helicopters to access, and no plane could land near the station. But a plane could fly OVER it. So the Navy agents put on special harnesses. The harnesses were attached to a line that was carried skyward by a huge balloon.

The plan was for a U.S. aircraft with a hook-on attached to its nose to fly over and snag the line hanging from the balloon.

The officers would find themselves suddenly YANKED into the air, and from there, they could be hauled into the plane.

I know, I know, it sounds like the stupidest plan ever. And guess what? It worked perfectly!

Moral: I'm still too amazed at that airplane trick to think of a moral to this story.

Hang on—I think I hear an ice cream truck. Gotta go!

WEIRD Assignments

Agents can get mixed up in all sorts of wacky things. For instance, in the 1950s, the CIA director ordered his spies to investigate UFOs. The director's reason was that if aliens existed, it would be REALLY important for the United States to know about them.

You know, I was going to make fun of that idea . . . but it actually makes sense!

I'll bet that if I look, I can find some other spy assignments that are peculiar. Hey, here's something: when a spy gets what's called a "wet job," that means it is a mission that might involve people bleeding.

So if *you're* assigned to a wet job, dress appropriately. For example, bloodstains don't show up as well on dark clothing. And waterproofed fabrics won't stain at all!

But then there is the WRONG kind of a wet job. Did you know that when world leaders visit the United States, they pee and poop? It's true! And if someone were to collect some of the pee and poop, THAT would be intelligence! By analyzing a person's number 2, you can find out what his health is like. So, when possible, that's exactly what CIA agents do! (Consider that a warning!)

CHEMICAL AGENTS

Cleisthenes of Sicyon was an ancient Greek leader who liked to conquer other cities. But at least the headman did it in creative ways. To take over one town, Cleisthenes had his agents put a powerful laxative in its water. As the poor townspeople ran around, desperately looking for a place to poop, Cleisthenes' soldiers waltzed in and took over.

Ooh, here's another *really* wet job. In 1950, an American agent named Edward Lansdale (see p. 138) was in the Philippines working against a Communist group. Knowing that there were local superstitions about vampires, Lansdale spread rumors that bloodsuckers were out and about. Scary!

After Lansdale's Filipino allies killed a Communist in battle, the American would have the dead man's throat punctured and his blood drained. And when the Communist's body was later found, this would spook everyone . . . *especially* the Communists!

Now here are some other weird intelligence assignments.

EVE, THE ORIGINAL DOUBLE AGENT

You've heard the story of Adam and Eve. No espionage there, right?

Wrong! The serpent that gets Eve to bite the apple is actually an enemy agent working under the "cover" of a reptile. This scaly agent "flips" Eve to his side when he gets her to eat the fruit of knowledge.[1] And then Eve gets Adam to do the same thing! So that means that Eve was tricked into becoming an agent for the other side without even knowing it!

HOW TO DESTROY A WORLD LEADER'S BEARD

As the leader of Cuba, Fidel Castro has been a world-famous enemy of the United States for decades. And to get back at the bearded Cuban dictator, the CIA came up with a kooky plan. Castro was going to be traveling, and it was believed that he would put his shoes in the hallway to get them shined. The idea was that CIA agents would then take the

---

1. You could call this a "false flag deception" (see p. 225).

shoes and sprinkle a chemical powder in them—and this powder would make all of his hair fall out.

Once Castro's famous beard dropped off his face, he would be without his macho symbol of leadership! And then either Castro's nation would rebel against him or he would just quit.

But since Castro cancelled his trip, we'll never know if this would have worked!

SPORTS ESPIONAGE?

BASEBALL

Think about your favorite sport. Got it? Whatever that sport is, I can guarantee you that it's filled with informants, double agents, and backstabbers! (Exception: golf. There are no spies in golf, because they can't stay awake.)

I mean, have you ever noticed how football coaches cover their mouths with clipboards so no one can see what play they're calling? And *baseball* is even worse! Teams constantly spy on each other to steal the "signs" that coaches use to communicate with their players on the field. And I haven't even told you about Moe Berg yet!

Moe Berg was both a genius and a pretty good baseball player. After he graduated from Princeton, Berg was signed by the Dodgers. For the next 16 years, he played major league baseball. But Berg was never a very good hitter, batting a lifetime .243 average. As one teammate said, "[Berg] can speak seven languages, but he can't hit in any of them."

It turns out that Berg's baseball career was a cover for the fact that Berg was an American spy! What use is a baseball spy? As "the brainiest player in baseball," Berg could speak fluent Japanese. So in 1934, he traveled with Babe Ruth on an American All-Star baseball tour to Japan. And between games, Berg put on a kimono, hid a movie camera under it, and climbed the stairs to one of the tallest buildings in Tokyo. There he filmed and photographed Japanese military installations for U.S. intelligence!

After leaving baseball in 1939, Berg worked for the FBI and the CIA. Because he was also fluent in German, Berg parachuted behind enemy lines at least once. He was also sent on missions to help sabotage a Nazi project to build an atomic bomb.

Through it all, Berg kept up an eccentric reputation. He was known to go on secret missions while still wearing his CIA-issue watch, he read up to 15 newspapers a day, and he was notorious for dropping his gun. (Berg once fumbled his firearm right into the lap of a fellow train passenger!)

Berg continued doing intelligence work in his sixties, but his full story will never be known. He was supposed to write a book about his adventures, but the editor he was going to work with let slip that he thought Moe Berg was Moe from "The Three Stooges." Berg was not amused, and the book was never written.

HORSEBACK RIDING

One of my favorite sporty-spy stories has to do with horseback riding. Yasumasa Fukushima was born to a Japanese samurai family in the 1800s. Growing up, he learned the importance of both spying and riding a horse. As a young man, Fukushima was sent to Germany to gather intelligence as a diplomat. He already had a reputation for doing brave, even foolhardy things. But people were still surprised when Fukushima announced he intended to ride a horse from Berlin, Germany, to the east coast of Russia—a distance of 9,000 miles!

Since that's more than twice the distance from California to New York, no one took Fukushima seriously—until he rode off. His daring trip attracted so much attention that the Russians didn't notice that Fukushima took notes along his entire journey. Yep, he was *spying*!

And when Japan and Russia went to war in 1904, guess who was an important officer of military intelligence? Fukushima!

And guess who won the war? Japan!

SAILING/YACHTING

Yes, spies can be behind a catcher's mask, on horseback, or even on a sailboat. For example, one of the biggest events in sailing (a.k.a. yachting) is the America's Cup. It's only held once every four years, so the sailors have plenty of time to secretly watch each other. Of special interest to yachters is what kind of keel (the part of the boat underwater) their opponents will have.

To prevent anyone from seeing their keel, sailors seal off their docks and hire armed guards. In 1992, an interesting bit of espionage happened with a New Zealand boat that was being guarded. A scuba diver named Amir Pishdad swam near the yacht. He was going to spy on it! Pishdad took a deep breath and left his air tank on the bottom so his bubbles wouldn't give him away. But as he was photographing the boat's keel, Pishdad was seen!

Two diver-guards who had been hired for just this situation dove into the water. Since Pishdad didn't have his tank, he couldn't swim off, and so he was easily caught. Talk about embarrassing!

FROM WATER TO AIR

When people fail to make their car payments, their cars can be repossessed. That means that people working for the bank or car dealership come and "steal" the auto back. This same thing works with jets. And because aircraft can cost millions of dollars, there's a lot of money at stake with them.

That's where repossession companies like Sage-Popovich, Inc., come in. Over the years, its employees have "stolen" back over 1,000 jets. But because aircraft are so valuable, repossessing them is tough. So repo agents have to combine the trickiness of an intelligence agent with the flying ability of a top pilot. Their unofficial rule is "Don't ask, don't tell—just get the airplane back."

The problem is that it's easy to quickly hide a jet someplace far away—like another continent! So jet repo agents have to be flexible. They need to know the layouts of airports, how to get their crews in, and where the jets are actually located. But the good news is that once the jet is found, the doors are usually unlocked. (Jet owners just assume that since their aircraft are at secure airports, they're safe!) Not only that, but you don't even need keys to start most jets. Sweet!

One repo pilot described an interesting job at a Paris airport. The jet was surrounded by orange cones, which we can agree is not very good security. (Orange cones can't stop anyone!) Inside the jet, a legal order was taped to the cockpit door. It commanded that the plane was not to be flown until its owners paid their fuel bills. No problem! As the repo pilot said, "It was all in French, so I just tore it off."

But airport security arrived and arrested the repo pilot. He had to leave the country and then re-enter by train. This time, he had the jet re-registered as an American plane.

Going to the airport, he found the jet again, only to find its fuel tanks had been drained. Drat!

Seeing that a nearby jet was being refueled, the repo pilot quickly bought enough to get him to Iceland, powered up the jet, and flew the now "American" plane out of Paris. Nice work! And it allowed the jet repo agent to do one of his favorite activities—imagining the expressions on the other pilots' faces when they realize their plane is gone!

PROJECT MINDREADING

You may have heard that the CIA experimented with ESP and mind reading to steal secrets from other countries. It's true! There was a program like this called "Remote Viewing" that was cancelled in 1995. It was run by a former Special Forces commander named Colonel John Alexander. He spent years trying to convince the military that mind reading was possible.

As part of the "Remote Viewing" program, Alexander brought in witches and psychics. But he was not impressed by the witches at all, saying they "lacked discipline and protocols."

This is sort of like looking for aliens—it's easy to make fun of. But what if there ARE psychics? Then we spies had better know about them!

But when the "mad scientists" from DARPA (see p. 36) was brought in to evaluate the CIA program, it took them just a few hours to realize something important: mind reading doesn't work! Rats.

IF YOU CAN'T BEAT THEM, STEAL FROM THEM

In 1969, the people of Israel were a little worried. One of its neighbors, Egypt, had just set up a new radar station that gave away the location of Israeli aircraft.

The Israelis considered bombing the radar station, but that seemed like a waste of expensive new technology—even if it was the enemy's! So one night, a group of special agents were quickly flown into Egypt. They took over the radar installation. Then they dismantled it and had two "heavy-lift" helicopters fly off with it!

KEEP AN EYE ON THE WEATHER

In addition to secretly watching people, a good spy observes MANY things—like the weather! Just knowing which way the wind is blowing can be useful. According to legend, a battle was waged in China over 2,000 years ago. Leading one side was a brilliant man named Liang Zhuge. And Liang Zhuge's army was defeated! Panic-stricken, his soldiers fled certain death by crossing a river.

Liang Zhuge looked at his men. They were hungry, outnumbered, bone-tired, and facing complete destruction. On the other side of the river, the enemy happily made camp, secure in the knowledge that they could destroy Liang's army first thing in the morning. (Destroying one's enemies at dawn is always a good feeling!)

But Liang Zhuge didn't become the leader by being a fool! And as he looked across the river, he noted that the wind was blowing TOWARD the enemy camp. And so that evening, Liang Zhuge ordered his men to light hundreds and hundreds of paper lanterns. And after darkness fell, Liang ordered his men to release the flocks of paper lanterns into the night air.

As the lanterns floated happily across the river, Liang had his archers get their bows and arrows ready. And as the lanterns landed on the enemy camp and set everything on fire, soldiers rushed to the river to escape the flames and get water!

And that's when Liang's archers let loose a hailstorm of arrows that decimated the enemy. The survivors fled, leaving their supplies behind, and Liang won the first battle ever decided by paper lanterns. (Just imagine what he could have done with a bunch of flashlights!)

KOOKIEST DEAD SPY AGENCY

There were a lot of spies in East Germany between 1945 and 1989. I'll bet you couldn't throw a schnitzel in that country without hitting a secret agent. (But why are you throwing schnitzels?)

After World War II ended in 1945, Germany was divided into two parts. West Germany was under the watch of the Allies (France, England, and the United States), while East Germany was taken over by Russia and turned into a Communist country.

The East German spy agency that was created was called the Stasi (1950–1989). It is possible that no spy agency in history ever spent more energy keeping an eye on its people than Stasi agents did. The following story shows the kooky lengths they would go to:

In the 1970s, the president of East Germany, Walter Ulbricht, kept getting hate mail. Specifically, every time Ulbricht's photo was in the paper, someone would cut it out, write "Big fat pig" across it, and mail it to him. How mean!

This bothered the president, so he asked the Stasi to look into it. Their solution:

1. The agents checked the postmark of these letters and saw that they came from Dresden, which was in East Germany.

2. The agents planted a story about Ulbricht in the country's biggest newspaper.

3. The agents stopped all newspapers delivered to Dresden. Then the agents used invisible ink to print a different number on the BACK of the newspaper page where Ulbricht's photo was. (This number was different for every newspaper subscriber!) How many newspapers did they have to do this to? Well, over 500,000 people lived in the city!

4. The agents waited.

Sure enough, Ulbricht got another "Big fat pig" letter. The Stasi agents analyzed the invisible ink. Then they went through their files and identified a matching newspaper subscriber. He was the guilty one!

Sure, the mission was a success. But think of all the work and money that it cost the East Germans to identify someone who was sending silly messages in the mail!

BECOMING A PRO

You know what makes me mad? I keep asking the CIA to be my Facebook friend, and I keep getting denied! What a rip-off. But despite this injustice, it's possible that you—like me—want to pursue a career in intelligence.[1]

So what are the steps to becoming a real spy? Here are some things that couldn't hurt:

PLAY A LOT OF THE BOARD GAME STRATEGO. It's pretty fun, especially when you use the "Spy" piece to assassinate your opponent's leader.

AVOID GROWING TOO MUCH. The MI5 (p. 293) once listed the perfect height for a male spy as 5 feet 8 inches. Any taller, and the agent might stick out. Any shorter, and the agent wouldn't be able to see over a crowd!

---

1. Either that, or you're making a Doomsday Device as revenge for having read this far.

DON'T POST INSULTING OR DUMB MATERIAL ONLINE. This includes publishing mean YouTube comments and posting photos on Facebook of you bungee jumping without a bungee cord. When people check up on you, the LESS online information they can find, the better.

Of course, even big-shot spies make these kinds of mistakes. In 2009, John Sawers was getting ready to become head of Britain's MI6 (a.k.a. the Secret Intelligence Service). Then his wife posted items about their family on her Facebook page—things like where they lived and worked, who their friends were, and where the family went on vacation. AND she even posted a picture of Sawers wearing a Speedo.

Talk about blowing someone's cover!

Bonus "Oops!": The MI6 is also in charge of Great Britain's cyber-security.

WORK ON BEING AMBIDEXTROUS. Think of how impressed the other spy wannabes will be when they find out you can shoot poison darts equally well with either hand![2]

GET GOOD GRADES. Do you know how many spies didn't go to college? Me neither, but I don't think there are

---

2. And that way, if one hand is injured, you're still dangerous.

very many. And while you're in college, take at least a few international studies courses.

LEARN A FOREIGN LANGUAGE (or three!). No pressure, but Sir Richard Burton (1821–1890) was one of the most brilliant spies ever. Part of his success came from the fact that he learned 35 languages.

STAY OUT OF TROUBLE. If you have a gambling problem or a criminal background, you probably won't be hired. My best advice is to hang out exclusively with other people who have read this book.

As a future agent, you should also know the different categories of secrecy. American agencies break it down this way:

Confidential: Whatever you're looking at is kind of, sort of, secret.

Secret: Anything labeled "secret" is *definitely* secret.

Top Secret: This is so secret, it couldn't be any MORE secret!

Cosmic: I lied. Things CAN be more secret! Cosmic secrets are the tip-top secret level of secrecy used by NATO (an alliance of countries including the United States).

Other countries have their own classifications of secrecy. British material could once be classified Most Secret. And as if that wasn't good enough, the most sensitive level was Hush Most Secret.

I hope you agree with me that it's not very impressive when spies use the word "hush." And there's another category for secrets that can only be whispered:

Ears Only: This must be the most secret of them all! The category of Ears Only is given to any information that is so TOTALLY outrageously secret, it must not be written down. Ears Only has to be *said,* and then, only in super-safe areas that have been debugged.

YOUR APPLICATION

Okay, so now you're ready to apply to an intelligence agency. Good luck! Your hiring process will go like this:

1. PAPERWORK! You'll have to turn in LOTS of forms. The spy agency will especially want to know if you're an honest person who is loyal to your country. In addition to the usual questions about your past, they'll REALLY want to know if you've ever gotten in trouble for hacking. (And hopefully, you haven't . . . or if you have, you're so good that it's a plus!)

2. TAKE PSYCHOLOGICAL TESTS! The agency wants to know if you are a stable, organized person.

You will also be scored in personality categories like

- 👁 Are you outgoing? A show-off? Really shy? Insane?
- 👁 Are you open to new experiences? Are you closed to old experiences? Insane?
- 👁 Are you a trusting and agreeable person? Paranoid? Gullible? Insane?

3. TAKE A LIE-DETECTOR TEST! Obviously,

the idea is to find out how honest you are. But just as important is how you deal with pressure. One of the favorite tricks that polygraph questioners love to play is this: during the exam, the questioner will say, "And

now, this is the MOST IMPORTANT QUESTION on the exam!"

4. THE BACKGROUND INVESTIGATION.

This is where your friends, relatives, former co-workers and fellow students will get asked things like

- Does she have any "issues"?
- Would you consider her trustworthy?
- Does she know any foreigners? Who? How often does she see them?
- Has she read any books by Bart King? She has? Don't you love that guy? You don't!? Are you insane?

YOU'RE HIRED! (NOW YOU'RE A MORON.)

Let's say you got the job. Congratulations! Now you get to start learning some SECRETS. But being a spy with top secret clearance has its dangers! When an intelligence expert named Daniel Ellsberg received his top security clearance, another agent warned him about the stages he would go through:

1. You're excited by all of the top secret things you're learning. Being a spy RULES!

2. You feel like a fool for the times you criticized leaders like the president. They had top secret info and you *didn't* . . . and you thought *you* knew better?

3. After about two weeks, you think anyone who doesn't have a top secret clearance like yours is an idiot. After two more years of this, you can't learn from anybody who doesn't have top secret clearance. That's because you're always thinking, *"He doesn't know what I know."* So no matter how smart the experts are, you ignore them!

4. You are now a moron.

Of course, if you know you might become a moron, you can prevent it from happening! And another good way to avoid becoming a moron is to travel to secret spots where you can study intelligence with the best spies out there.

One place you might be able to get into is Disneyland's super-secret Club 33. It's in the New Orleans Square part of Disneyland. Just go to the Blue Bayou Restaurant and look for the "33 Royal Street" address. You'll only see a door there—but if you're a club member, that door will open! "Normal" people have to pay as much as $30,000 to join the club and there's a 14-year waiting list! But with your security clearance, you should be able to go in and enjoy Club 33's amazing [*description deleted by Disney security*].

SECRET RESEARCH

In Rome is a place called the Vatican Secret Archives. That's its real name! It has 52 miles of shelving and documents and stuff that dates back thousands of years![3]

---

3. Despite the name, *anyone* can visit the Vatican Secret Archives and request material.

CONSOLATION PRIZE

If you can't get a job as a spy, but you like badges and dangerous work, move to Texas. With about 75,000 law officers, Texas has one of the highest ratios of police to population in the world. In addition to sheriffs and police, Texas also has armed law officers working for school districts, the State Insurance Department, the Lottery Commission, the Pharmacy Board, the State Board of Dental Examiners, and even a bunch of water districts.

It wasn't until Texas *foot doctors* requested their own law-enforcement officer that something had to give. Thankfully, someone pointed out that foot doctors don't really *need* their own police agency . . . unless criminal hangnails are a bigger problem than anyone realizes!

Hang on. I just got an email . . . and *yes!* Who's got two thumbs and is the CIA's new Facebook friend?

AGENCIES!

Hey, maybe you're not sure what spy agency you want to work for. It's smart to be careful! After all, you don't want to get stuck with a mean boss. Like a candy maker! They can be the most ruthless spymasters around. You know, like in Roald Dahl's book *Charlie and the Chocolate Factory*? In it, Grandpa Joe explains why Willy Wonka shut down his first chocolate factory. It was because of all the dirty, stinking spies!

"All of the other chocolate makers, you see, had begun to grow jealous of the wonderful candies that Mr. Wonka was making, and they started sending in spies to steal his secret recipes." (More on Roald Dahl on p. 239.)

To solve his problem, Willy Wonka hires Oompa-Loompas to run his candy factories. Wonka had rescued these little people from the vicious beasts of Loompaland. In return, the Oompa-Loompas were grateful, loyal, and could keep a secret. Plus, they could sing!

But real candy companies like Nestlé and Mars[1] don't have that option. And since these candy companies are bitter competitors, they always want to know what the OTHER one is doing. What new candies are coming out? What ad campaigns will they have? What will the recipes be?

Without Oompa-Loompas to help, Nestlé and Mars choose another path. They hire ex-CIA agents to snag secret documents, keep an eye on rival leaders, and rip the lid off of their archenemy's hidden operations. It's a huge chocolate war out there!

Part of the appeal of trying to learn a competitor's candy recipe is that it's impossible to patent the ingredients for a chocolate bar. In other words, if you figured out the perfect way to make the most delicious candy bar in the world, someone could copy it and legally make it themselves.

For example, the Hershey Company makes the coconut candy bar called Mounds. And way back in the 1950s, the

---

1. Nestlé makes Smarties, Butterfingers, and Kit Kats. Mars makes Snickers, M&Ms, and, uh, Mars bars.

Mars company "borrowed" the recipe. Then Mars made a coconut bar they called "Bounty," and they started selling it in Great Britain. Can you believe it? And that's why Hershey's doesn't sell Mounds in Great Britain.

But what about the chocolate spies? Don't they feel a little silly? Maybe, but the pay is sweet! It turns out that a government spy makes good money. But a spy working for a private company can make TWICE as much or more. MUCH more! So there is a huge temptation for agents to get intelligence training from a government, work for a few years, and then quit and work for private spy agencies.

In Washington, D.C., alone, there are dozens of spy firms that employ thousands of ex-FBI, ex-CIA, ex-Secret Service, and ex-MI5 agents. There is even a private agency that specializes only in Russian agents! And these private agencies then get hired by big corporations.

What kind of big corporation hires spies? ALL big corporations. I've only been using candy companies as an example because I like candy. But pretty much EVERY company on the planet has competitors. So if they can gain an edge by spying, then they will!

Look, I'm not saying that every single company hires spies. Just the ones that can afford to! But enough about *private* spy agencies. Let's look at the different U.S. spy agencies!

TOO MANY SPIES ARE IN THE KITCHEN

When the Revolutionary War was fought in 1776, the United States had no organized spy network. And by the War of 1812 began, it STILL didn't have one! It wasn't until 1885 that an actual U.S. military intelligence department was set up.

The department consisted of one officer and one clerk. These two agents gathered most of their information by reading newspapers—which was actually a pretty good approach!

Although it got off to a slow start, the United States made up for lost time. The country spends well over $50 billion a year gathering intelligence. And all that cash is spread out over SEVENTEEN different intelligence agencies in the federal government. Yep, there are 17 of them, and they're all competing for money as well as the honor of being the president's "go to" spy group.

Because there are so many, no one has ever been able to name all of them. So here—for the first time ever!—are all of the American intelligence agencies.

NATIONAL SECURITY AGENCY (NSA): This is the BIGGEST American intelligence agency! The NSA is in charge of breaking and making codes and waging "information warfare." The NSA is so secret, its nickname is No Such Agency. And it's so big, the NSA measures its computer space in acres. **ACRES!**

NSA headquarters are in Maryland, and if you're trying to drive there, you'll know when you get close. That's because the NSA jams electronic signals. So your car's GPS will trap you into a bunch of U-turns!

The people at NSA are usually very good at math and are often shy. Shy people are sometimes called "shoe-gazers" because they don't make eye contact. Instead they look down at their shoes! So here is an NSA joke:

Q. How can you tell the extrovert at NSA?

A. He's the one looking at someone *else's* shoes.

CENTRAL INTELLIGENCE AGENCY (CIA):

This organization is in charge of general intelligence outside the United States. (Its motto: "Human intelligence on foreign targets.") Nobody knows how many employees the CIA has, but there may be around 20,000. The CIA has only been around since 1947. But if it *had* existed before World War II, the Japanese attack on Pearl Harbor might have been foiled. It turns out that the U.S. government had plenty of information ABOUT the upcoming attack, but there wasn't anyone around to pull the different sources together!

But its agents have learned a lot since 1947. Here's how tricky today's CIA is: to send fan mail to it, you address your letter to "Langley, Virginia." But there is NO town or village in Virginia known as Langley! Pretty sly, huh? Ha! Nobody will ever find the CIA headquarters!

Unless, of course, you happen to be driving on the Washington Parkway in Virginia. If you are, you'll see highway signs marking the exit for the secret spy agency.

What's weird is that the CIA has no law enforcement powers. So while a CIA agent can spy, commit espionage, and even assassinate people, he has no authority to make an arrest. And if a CIA spymaster suspects one of his own agents is a traitor, he has to call in the FBI to investigate him!

FEDERAL BUREAU OF INVESTIGATION

(FBI): These agents don't spy, but they do try to CATCH foreign spies and American double agents.

"MI" STANDS FOR "MILITARY INTELLIGENCE"

Formed in 1909, the MI6 is the United Kingdom's international spy agency. (Sort of like the CIA.) The most famous MI6 employee is fictional—Bond . . . James Bond. The UK also has MI5, which is something like the American FBI. It's in charge of all internal security threats.

DEFENSE INTELLIGENCE AGENCY (DIA):

The U.S. Department of Defense (DOD) supervises the U.S. armed forces and is in charge of national security. If you've ever seen the Pentagon, the DOD is the main tenant there. And the Defense Intelligence Agency is its spy group.

NATIONAL GEOSPATIAL-INTELLIGENCE AGENCY (NGA):

This agency makes and analyzes maps and photographs.

NATIONAL RECONNAISSANCE OFFICE

(NRO): This bureau provides satellite photos and graphics to other agencies.

DRUG ENFORCEMENT ADMINISTRATION (DEA): This enforcement agency provides intelligence inside the United States having to do with drugs.

DEPARTMENT OF HOMELAND SECURITY (DHS): After the terrorist attack known as 9/11, this department was formed as a special branch intended to foil terrorists.

Also, the **Coast Guard** and each branch of the military (**Air Force, Army, Marines, Navy**) has its own intelligence agency, as do the departments of **State, Energy,** and **Treasury.**

Can all these spy agencies be trusted to fully cooperate with each other? NO! In fact, many of them are known to keep secrets to themselves and compete with their "rivals." But in the aftermath of September 11, 2001, the **Office of the Director of National Intelligence (ODNI)** was created. This accomplished two important things:

1. It created a director who supposedly oversees all these different branches.

2. That director sits down with the president every morning to go over top secret stuff.

★ *Can You Guess?* Where do you think most of the billions of dollars budgeted for spy work in the United States goes? Answer below![2]

In 2010, the U.S. military got something called the **U.S. Cyber Command (CYBERCOM)**, and it can be included as the newest intelligence agency. As its name suggests, the Cyber Command is charged with keeping government computers safe from attack—and maybe preparing for a little attacking of its own.

The Cyber Command also has its own government seal. In a playful move, the CYBERCOM seal has a code on its inner ring that reads "9ec4c12949a4f31474f299058ce2b22a." This prompted people to try and decode the message, and their guesses were way more interesting than the real answer.[3]

"If you can read this, send us a job application!"

"drowssap."

"Access denied."

"Made you look!"

"Be sure to drink your Ovaltine."

"If the intelligence community is a family, think of us as the uncle no one talks about."

"I can has cheezburger?"

"In God We Trust. (Everybody else gets monitored.)"

"You just got pwned."

---

2. Spy satellites and listening devices.

3. "CYBERCOM plans, coordinates, integrates, synchronizes, and conducts activities to: direct the operations and defense of specified Department of Defense information networks and prepare to, and when directed, conduct full-spectrum military cyberspace operations in order to enable actions in all domains, ensure freedom of action in cyberspace for the U.S. and its allies, and deny the same to our adversaries."

MOST EMPLOYMENT OPPORTUNITIES

Because most spies don't like to be identified and counted, it's impossible to know for sure what country has the most agents. The KGB was the intelligence agency of the old Soviet Union (1917–1991). It was so colossal, the KGB was bigger than all the Western spy agencies *combined*. In the 1980s, estimates are that the KGB employed about 400,000 people.[4] But today, China is the new record holder. In 2005, two Chinese diplomats defected from the country. The men claimed that China has 1,000 spies and informers in Canada alone. If that's true, population ratios suggest that there are over 9,000 Chinese spies in the United States!

China has also set up about 3,000 fake and semi-fake companies worldwide. These companies then work as "fronts" for Chinese spies. If that sounds sort of cheap, the CIA set up its own airline called Air America back in 1950. For the next 25 years, Air America pretended to be a regular passenger airline. And it was huge! Between 1961 and 1975, it was the world's largest commercial airline. And Air America probably had the world's toughest pilots, too, as they were almost all ex-military.

With this set-up, Air America actually specialized in moving spies, spy supplies, informants, diplomats, and anything

---

4. Today, the KGB has been replaced by three different Russian intelligence agencies.

else that might be intelligence related. Air America's motto?
"Anything, Anywhere,
Anytime—Professionally."

Oops—hang on.
One of my agents
just handed me a top secret text message, sent by carrier
pigeon! It states that 7 out of 10 of the world's spam
messages come from Russia, Ukraine, and Estonia.

This is great news! Now where's my passport? I'm sorry
to leave you, but I'm going on a mission to eradicate those
spammers once and for all. So by the time you read this, the
spam menace will be ancient history![5]

---

5. And if it's *not*, could someone rescue me from whatever Estonian jail spam
fighters get thrown into?

TERMINOLOGY!

Agent provocateur: A spy whose job is to MAKE trouble and then blame it on someone else. Example: in the 1930s, Japanese agents provocateurs destroyed things and then blamed the Chinese. This gave Japan an excuse to attack China.

Angel: An enemy agent. "Look out, there's an angel behind you—Aaaaah!"

Babysitter: Either a bodyguard OR a person hired by your parents to ensure you don't engage in sabotage.

Bang and burn: Sabotage operation.

Brush Contact: Two spies pass each other on the street. While brushing past each other, they secretly pass documents or other information to each other. Once in a while, to crack each other up, the spies will pass an actual brush. (Hey, nobody said that spies don't have a good sense of humor!)

Chicken feed: Useless information. Example: "After prying open Debbie's diary, I learned that she likes Justin Bieber. Chicken feed!"

Cobbler: A person who can fake important documents like passports, driver licenses, and report cards.

Cold War: After World War II ended in 1945, a constant state of hostility called the Cold War began between the Soviet Union (a country that has since been divided into Russia and 13 other nations) and the United States and Western Europe. Since the Cold War was being fought among spies on all sides, it was an "intelligence war."

Cover story: This is an alibi. It can be as simple as explaining why someone is in the office late at night ("I forgot how to tell time!") or as complex as an entire fake identity ("My name is John Doe. I forgot how to tell time!")

Crippie: A cryptologist, or person who makes secret codes. From them, we get the rhyme, "The crippie crept into the crypt, encrypted, then crapped and crept out again."

Cutout: A person who serves as a go-between for a spymaster and his spies.

Dead drop: A secret location for leaving or picking up secret documents. Not to be confused with "drop dead," which is a not-so-secret insult.

Discard: Spy slang for an agent who is betrayed to protect (or get) a more valuable source.

Doomed spy: Also known as a "discard," this is a spy who is allowed to be caught in order to protect more valuable agents.

Double agent: A spy who pretends to work for one side while actually working for the other.

Dry cleaning: Trying to discover if you're being followed by turning down dead end streets, or speeding way up and then slowing way down.

Ears only: If you have a really important secret, don't write it down. Only whisper it to your trusted colleagues.

L-pill: A pill used by agents to commit suicide if they are captured. Example: "Timmy, don't let her have those L-pills! Oh, they're just Lifesavers?"

Mole: A spy who has burrowed deep into an enemy's stronghold and passes on secret information to the country he's working for.

Rolled-up: Used to describe an operation that has been discovered. Once its cover has been "blown," it has to be "rolled-up" or scrapped.

Safe house: A residence considered safe for spies to hang out in. *Tip*: when selecting a safe house, choose one that's close to a pizza parlor.

Spook: Spy

Tradecraft: The basic skills that a spy must possess. Although interesting, the world of tradecraft may not be quite as fun to play as the World of Warcraft.

SELECTED BIBLIOGRAPHY

Acocella, Nick. "Moe Berg: Catcher and Spy." ESPN.com, July 29, 2004.

"Ageing spies unable to use the Internet." London: *The Telegraph*, March 28, 2010.

Allen, Thomas B. *Declassified: 50 Documents That Changed History*. Washington, D.C.: National Geographic, 2008.

"Amy Elizabeth Thorpe: WWII's Mata Hari." Historynet.com.

Barboza, David, and John Markoff. "Researchers Trace Data Theft to Intruders in China." *The New York Times*, April 5, 2010.

Belfiore, Michael. *The Department of Mad Scientists: How DARPA Is Remaking Our World, from the Internet to Artificial Limbs*. New York: Smithsonian Books, 2009.

Brenner, Joël Glenn. "Chocolate Wars: The inspiration for Charlie and the Chocolate Factory." Slate.com, July 15, 2005.

Bridis, Ted. "Those tiger droppings may be a CIA microphone." *Oakland Tribune*, December 27, 2003.

Burnett, John. "In Texas, a Police Officer for Everyone?" National Public Radio, *Morning Edition,* October 9, 2009.

"The Champagne Spy." *Time*, November 23, 1070.

"Chevalier d'Eon." *The Independent,* April 19, 2006. http://www. independent.co.uk.

Clarke, Richard A., and Robert K. Knake. *Cyber War: The Next Threat to National Security and What to Do About It*. New York: Ecco/ HarperCollins, 2010.

Collins, Dennis, and the International Spy Museum. *Spying: The Secret History of History*. New York: Black Dog & Leventhal Publishing, 2004.

Collins, Nick. "Move over James Bond, you're too tall." London: *The Telegraph*, April 6, 2010.

DeMarco, Michael. "Belle Boyd." Encyclopedia Virginia. http:// encyclopediavirginia.org.

Drummon, Katie. "Army Wants Sensors to Nab Sweaty, Smelly Security Threats." Wired.com (Danger Room), April 26, 2010.

Ellsberg, Daniel. *Secrets: A Memoir of Vietnam and the Pentagon Papers.* New York: Penguin, 2003.

Espinoza, Cholene. "The Last Days of the Dragon Lady." *The New York Times,* May 7, 2010.

Fendel, Hillel. "Police Solve Case by Inventing 'Memory Machine.'" *Israel National News*, July 13, 2009.

Foer, Franklin. "Mossad." *Slate.com*, October 12, 1997.

Gjelten, Tom. "Cyber Insecurity: U.S. Struggles to Confront Threat." National Public Radio, *Morning Edition,* April 6, 2010.

———, "Cyberattack: U.S. Unready For Future Face Of War." National Public Radio, *Morning Edition,* April 7, 2010.

———, "Cyberwarrior Shortage Threatens U.S. Security." National Public Radio, *Morning Edition,* June 19, 2010.

Gladwell, Malcolm. "Pandora's Briefcase." *The New Yorker*, May 10, 2010.

Gottlieb, Zach. "Runaway Robots Hunted by the Mammals They Were Supposed to Replace." Wired.com (Danger Room), June 10, 2010.

Gray, Jefferson. "Holy Terror: The Rise of the Order of Assassins." Historynet.com, February 2010.

Green, Tim. "The history of steganography." NetworkWorld.com, September 8, 2009.

Hambling, David. "Attack of the Killer Dolphins (Maybe)." Wired.com (Danger Room), July 5, 2007.

———. "Psychic Spies, Acid Guinea Pigs, New Age Soldiers: the True *Men Who Stare at Goats*. Wired.com (Danger Room), November 6, 2009.

Harrison, David. "The secret war mission that inspired Goldfinger scene." London: *The Telegraph*, April 17, 2010.

Jackson, Vernice. "Mary Elizabeth Bowser." Women in History, http://www.lkwdpl.org.

Javers, Eamon. *Broker, Trader, Lawyer, Spy*. New York: Harper, 2010.

Joiner, Stephen. "Grab the Airplane and Go." *Air & Space Magazine*, May 1, 2010.

"J.R.R. Tolkien trained as British spy." London: *The Telegraph*, September 16, 2009.

Karacs, Sarah. "The Banalities and Betrayals of Life in East Germany." *Der Spiegel*, November 6, 2009.

Keefe, Patrick Radden. "The Trafficker." *The New Yorker*, February 8, 2010.

Kessler, Ronald. *Inside the CIA*. New York: Pocket Books, 1992.

———. *In the President's Secret Service*. New York: Crown Publishers, 2009.

Lineberry, Cate. "The Limping Spy." *Smithsonian*, February 1, 2007.

Lloyd, Mark. *The Guinness Book of Espionage*. New York: Da Capo Press, 1994.

Macintyre, Ben. *Operation Mincemeat*. New York: Harmony, 2010.

Melton, H. Keith, with Craig Piligian and Duane Swierczynski. *The Spy's Guide: Office Espionage*. Philadelphia: Quark Books, 2003.

Melton, H. Keith, and Robert Wallace. *The Official CIA Manual of Trickery and Deception*. New York: William Morrow, 2009.

Mendez, Antonio J. "A Classic Case of Deception." http://www.cia. gov, 1997.

Midgley, Carol. "Why do women make better spies than men? That's our little secret . . ." *TimesOnline*, December 3, 2003. http://www. timesonline.co.uk.

Nagy, John. *Ink: Spycraft of the American Revolution.* Yardley, Pennsylvania. Westholme Publishing, 2009.

"The Navy's Other Seals . . . and Dolphins." National Public Radio, *All Things Considered*, December 5, 2009.

Norton-Taylor, Richard. "Forgotten spy and escape artist extraordinaire comes in from the cold." Guardian.co.uk, March 31, 2010.

Owen, David. *Spies.* Richmond Hill, Ontario: Firefly Books, 2004.

Palmer Brian. "Go Go Gadget Beard!" *Slate.com*, February 17, 2010.

Perro, Ralph J. "Interviewing with an Intelligence Agency." Federation of American Scientists. http://www.fas.org.

"Pigeon held in India on suspicion of spying for Pakistan." Agence France-Presse, May 28, 2010.

Polmar, Norman, and Thomas B. Allen. *Spy Book: The Encyclopedia of Espionage, Second Edition.* New York: Random House, 2004.

———. Spy-Speak Archive. http://www.military.com.

Robins, Peter. "Contemporary bicycle-based self-defence." Telegraph. co.uk, November 8, 2008.

Rowe, Aaron. "10 Sci-Fi Weapons That Actually Exist." Wired.com (Danger Room), January 9, 2010.

Schactman, Noah. "Navy Dolphin Patrol Under Fire." Wired.com (Danger Room), January 28, 2009.

Schoenfeld, Gabriel. *Necessary Secrets: National Security, the Media, and the Rule of Law.* New York: Norton & Company, 2010.

Shane, Scott, and Charlie Savage. "In Ordinary Lives, U.S. Sees the Work of Russian Agents." *The New York Times*, June 28, 2010.

Shogol, Jeff. "Airborne bears to catch bin Laden, and other letters to the Pentagon." *Stars and Stripes*, March 16, 2010.

"Spy codenamed The White Rabbit to be honoured with blue plaque." *The Telegraph*, March 31, 2010.

Stajano, Frank, and Paul Wilson. "Understanding scam victims: seven principles for systems security." University of Cambridge Technical Report, August 2009.

Temple-Raston, Dina. "Spotting Lies: Listen, Don't Look." National Public Radio, *Morning Edition,* August 14, 2009.

"UK honors glow worm war heroes." CNN.com, November 24, 2004.

Vance, Ashley. "If Your Password Is *123456*, Just Make It *HackMe*." *The New York Times*, January 20, 2010.

Weinberger, Sharon. "Pentagon's Psychic Vision Revisited." Wired.com (Danger Room), June 28, 2007.

Worth, Robert. "New Hints of Skulduggery in Hamas Killing." *The New York Times*, February 16, 2010.

"WWII knicker spy Margery Booth photos to be auctioned." *BBC News,* September 10, 2010.

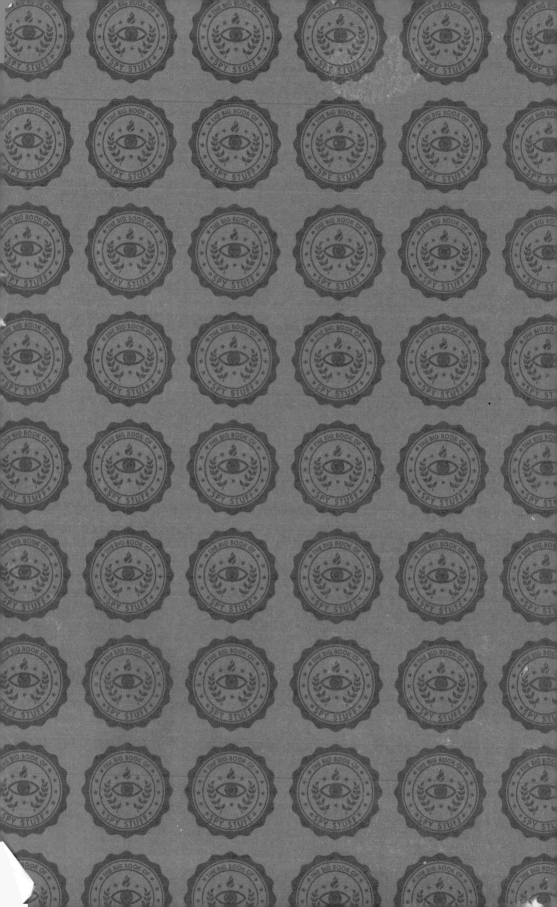